The Complete San Francisco Bay Area Sightseeing Guide

The Complete San Francisco Bay Area Sightseeing Guide

Rand Richards

Heritage House Publishers
San Francisco

First Printing September 1994

Cover design by Larry Van Dyke and Rand Richards.
Maps drawn by Larry Van Dyke.

Front and back cover photos and all photos inside the book are copyright © 1994 by Rand Richards. Back cover photos: mountain lion at the Lindsay Museum in Walnut Creek; the Camron-Stanford House at Lake Merritt in Oakland. Photo of the author © 1991 by Jeanine Reisbig.

Photo of the carousel horse on page 134 reproduced with the kind permission of the San Francisco Recreation and Parks Department and restoration artist Ruby Newman copyright © 1983, world rights reserved.

Printed in the United States of America

Heritage House Publishers
P.O. Box 194242
San Francisco, CA 94119

Library of Congress Cataloging-in-Publication Data

Richards, Rand
  The complete San Francisco Bay area sightseeing guide / Rand Richards.
      p.   cm.
  Includes index.
  ISBN 1-879367-02-5
  1. San Francisco Bay Area (Calif.)—Guidebooks.   I. Title.
F868.S156R49 1994
917.94'60453—dc20   94-25847
                                                              CIP

Dedicated to my friends in
the book business.

Contents

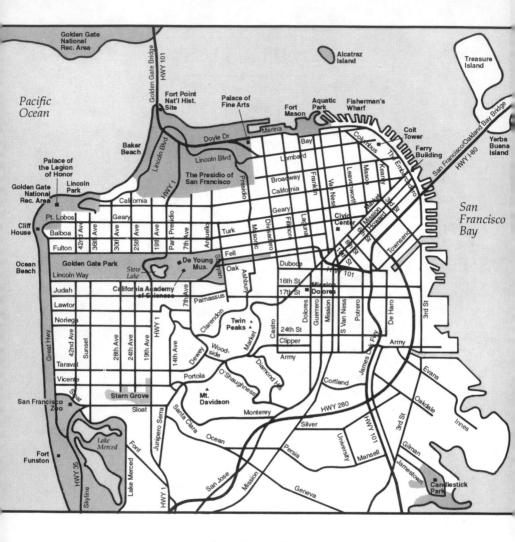

San Francisco

San Francisco's Northeast Corner →

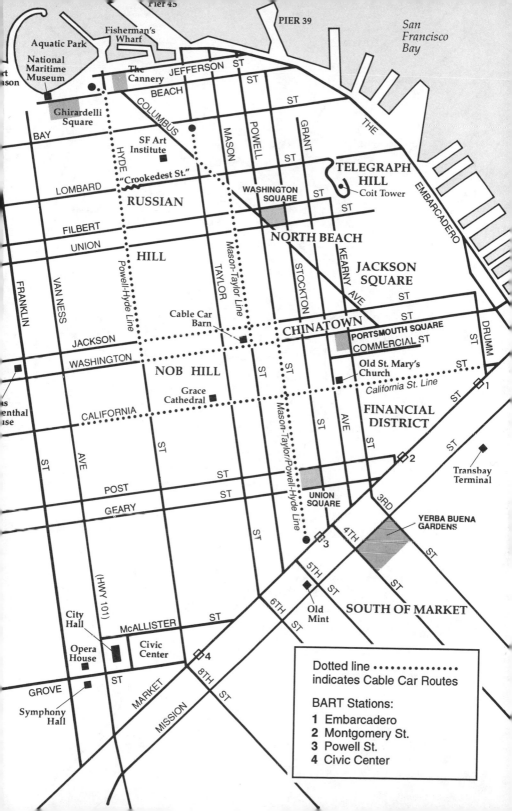

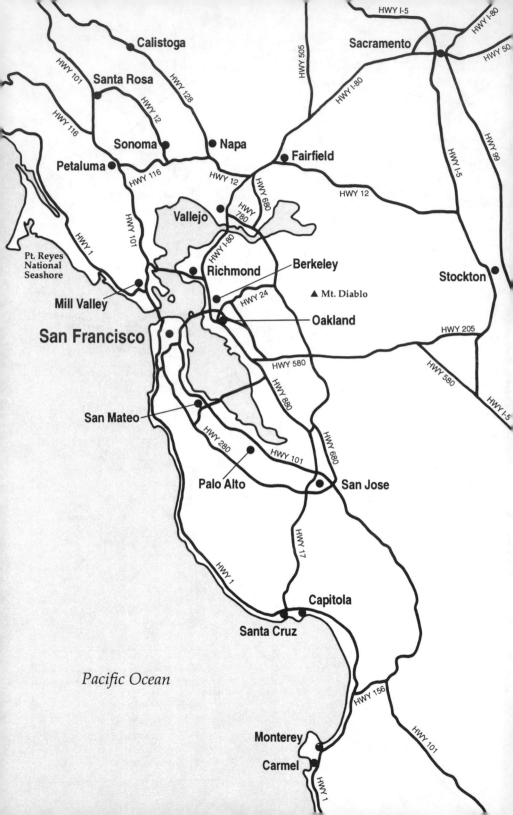

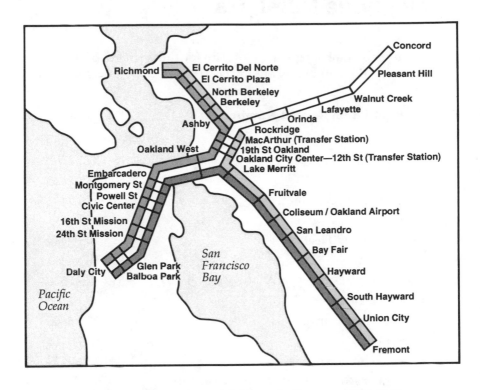

The Bay Area Rapid Transit System (BART)

Telephone Numbers

All phone numbers given below are for those dialed from San Francisco. All the numbers are in the **415** area code unless otherwise noted.

Transportation Related Numbers

AC Transit	1-800-559-INFO
Alameda/Oakland ferry	522-3300
AMTRAK	1-800-872-7245
Angel Island/Tiburon ferry	435-2131
BART	788-BART
Blue and Gold Fleet	705-5444
CalTrain	1-800-660-4287
County Connection (Contra Costa County)	1-510-676-7500
Golden Gate ferry	453-2100
Golden Gate Transit	332-6600
Greyhound	558-6789
Red & White Fleet	1-800-229-2784
San Francisco Municipal Railway (Muni)	673-MUNI
SamTrans	1-800-660-4BUS
Santa Clara County Transit	965-3100

Other Useful Numbers

Emergency (police, fire, ambulance)	911
Ambulance (non-emergency)	931-3900
California State Parks	456-1286
National Parks + GGNRA	556-0560
National Parks (weather and road conditions)	556-6030
National Weather Service forecast	364-7974
San Francisco Police Department (non-emergency)	553-0123
San Francisco Police Department (towed vehicles)	553-1235
Visitor Information Center (at Hallidie Plaza)	391-2000

Introduction

The San Francisco Bay Area's scenic beauty, cultural riches, and cosmopolitan diversity make it both one of the finest urban areas in the country to live in and one of the world's top travel destinations.

This book is designed as an easy-to-use guide to many of the museums, historic landmarks, parks, and other attractions that make the Bay Area the delightful place it is. If you, the reader, use this guide to "make the familiar new, and the new familiar," this book will have served its purpose.

A few general remarks about the places mentioned herein might save you from a wasted trip. Before you go it is always best to call ahead to verify that the museum is open and that the days and hours are the same as published here. San Francisco, in particular, is undergoing changes. Several major museums are closed or will soon be closing for seismic upgrading. Others, most notably the San Francisco Museum of Modern Art, are moving to the new Yerba Buena Gardens complex. Another thing to keep in mind, especially with smaller museums or historic landmarks — which are largely staffed by volunteers — is that they sometimes open later or close earlier than the posted hours.

Always call ahead if you are planning a visit on a holiday; many attractions that are open "daily" are closed Thanksgiving, Christmas, New Years Day, and some other holidays.

One final note: although many museums have "permanent" collections, even the objects in these tend to be rotated from time to time. So while specific items are mentioned in these pages, there is no guarantee that any particular item will be on view at the time of your visit.

How to Get Around

There are three major ways of getting around to see the sights and attractions mentioned in this book: by automobile, public transit, or commercial group tours. Driving your car certainly allows the most flexibility, and in a few instances it is the only way to get where you are going. Public transit is not as convenient, but with the highways becoming increasingly more congested, and with parking, especially in San Francisco, expensive or difficult to find, it has more appeal. Commercial tours provide a comfortable way to visit the top attractions, but because of time constraints only allow one to scratch the surface of what there is to see.

For those not wedded to the automobile, here is a little background information about local transit in general, and a listing of major alternatives for getting around the Bay Area.

The following applies to most of the transit companies:

- Exact change is required unless you have a transit pass.

- If you need a transfer, get it from the driver of the first bus or streetcar you board.

- Some transit agencies offer discounted one-day, three-day, seven-day, or monthly passes at significant savings over full-price single-trip tickets.

- Most companies have discounts for seniors, children, and the disabled.

- Many transit vehicles can accomodate the disabled, but it is best to call ahead to get specifics.

With nine major counties comprising the Bay Area, each with its own transit system, it has been difficult until recently to coordinate connections and transfers from one system to another. Progress has been made, however: an innovation has been the BART (Bay Area Rapid Transit) Plus pass, a value-added flash pass good on local buses connecting to BART. Contact BART for details.

San Francisco Transit and Parking

San Francisco Municipal Railway (Muni)

San Francisco has one of the better big city transit companies in the U.S., and perhaps because of that enjoys one of the highest per capita riderships. Coverage of the city through its streetcars and buses is comprehensive, and service is frequent. Of its 80 lines, 38 run at frequencies of 20 minutes or less until after midnight seven days a week. On major lines such as Geary or Mission, the frequency is 10 minutes or less.

Muni fares:

* Adults (18–35) $1.00.

* Youth (5–17), Seniors (65+), and Disabled, $0.35.

* Travel "Passports" (unlimited travel): 1-day $6.00; 3-day $10.00, 7-day $15.00. Monthly Fast Pass $35.00.

Individual rides can be purchased on board Muni vehicles. Transfers are valid for two uses in any direction for about two hours after issuance. "Passports" are available at the Visitor Information Center on the lower level of Hallidie Plaza near Powell and Market streets, at City Hall, and at a few other locations.

San Francisco Cable Cars

Also part of the Muni are San Francisco's trademark cable cars. There are three lines. All are in the northeast corner of the city. The Powell-Hyde line runs from Powell and Market to near Aquatic Park on the north waterfront. The Powell-Mason line also leaves from Powell and Market but terminates at Bay Street three blocks from Fisherman's Wharf. The California Street line extends from Van Ness Avenue to Market Street near the Embarcadero. Cable cars operate from 6 a.m. to about 1 a.m.

Cable car fares:

* Per person $2.00 (one way).

* Seniors and Disabled, from 9 p.m. to 7 a.m., $1.00.

Cable cars do not issue or accept transfers but Muni "Passports" are valid on them.

San Francisco Taxicabs

One option for seeing the sights in San Francisco is by taxicab. Meter rates start at $1.70 and increase $0.35 for each ⅙-mile after the first mile.

Some of the major cab companies and their phone numbers:

City Cab	(415) 468–7200
DeSoto Cab	(415) 673–1414
Luxor Cab	(415) 282–4141
National Cab	(415) 648–4444
Veteran's Cab	(415) 552–1300
Yellow Cab	(415) 626–2345

Parking in San Francisco

Street parking in San Francisco requires paying attention. Always check signs on the block and look for curb colors before parking and leaving your car.

Many streets, particularly in the downtown area, become towaway zones during morning and evening rush hours. If your car is towed it will cost you $100.00 or more for the tow plus the cost of the ticket. To retrieve your car you would need to go to a police station for a release and then to the towing company's lot to get your car. Avoid this expense and hassle by checking posted signs.

In most residential areas there is a two-hour limit for those without the proper neighborhood parking sticker, so watch for those signs, and for posted street-cleaning hours as well.

Generally you should never park in a space with a curb painted red, yellow, white, or blue. Especially not blue, because those are reserved for disabled drivers with identifying plates. Park in one of those without the proper plate on your dashboard and you will return to find a $275.00 ticket on your windshield. Also do not obstruct "cutouts," which are those scooped out depressions in the sidewalk, usually at corners, for wheelchair access. The same $275.00 fine applies if you obstruct one of those or if you park in a bus stop. Green-painted curbs are good for ten-minute parking only.

On hills, set the emergency brake, and be sure to cramp your car's wheels at an angle to the curb to prevent runaways. You can be ticketed for failing to do so.

In the downtown area you are probably better off parking in one of the city-owned parking garages. They are usually less expensive than privately-owned garages. The rates are kept low to encourage shoppers and visitors to come downtown. The eight major city-owned garages and their rates are:

	1 hr.	4 hrs.
1. Portsmouth Square	$1.00	$7.00
2. Golden Gateway	$3.00	$12.00
3. St. Mary's Square	$4.00	$17.00
4. Sutter-Stockton	$1.00	$5.00
5. Union Square	$2.00	$9.00
6. Ellis-O'Farrell	$1.00	$5.00
7. Fifth and Mission	$1.00	$5.00
8. Moscone Center	$1.00	$5.50

Bay Area Transit Systems

Bay Area Rapid Transit (BART)

BART is a rail system that connects San Francisco to the East Bay. There it extends north to Richmond and Concord and south as far as Fremont. It is primarily used by commuters, but its many stations connect with local transit that can get you to your ultimate destination. (See BART map on p. xi.)

BART trains run daily: Monday - Friday, 4 a.m. to midnight; Saturdays, 6 a.m. to midnight; Sundays, 8 a.m. to midnight. Trains run at 7- to 30-minute intervals.

Fares range from $0.80 to a maximum of $3.00, depending on distance traveled. You must purchase a ticket before boarding. All

BART stations, besides having excellent maps and fare charts, have ticket and change machines. (The machines change coins or $1 bills.) You can buy a ticket (or farecard) for the exact amount, or with more value added for use on other trips. When you enter the turnstile you insert your farecard in front. It then whisks it to the top, opening the barrier. Keep your farecard — you will need it to exit. To exit, insert your farecard as before. If your fare is exact the machine will keep your card. If you have value left over retrieve the card for later use.

Ferries

Below are the major San Francisco Bay ferries, their departure points, and their destinations:

- Alameda/Oakland ferry:
  From San Francisco's Ferry Building or PIER 39 to Oakland's Jack London Square and Alameda's Main Street terminal.

- Angel Island/Tiburon ferry:
  Travels between Tiburon and Angel Island State Park.

- Blue and Gold Fleet:
  Departs Pier 39. A 75-minute narrated sightseeing cruise of San Francisco Bay.

- Golden Gate ferry:
  Commuter ferry line from the Ferry Building to Sausalito and Larkspur in Marin County.

- Red & White Fleet:
  Departs Pier 41 and 43½ in San Francisco. Offers one-hour sightseeing cruises of the bay, and service to Alcatraz, Muir Woods (via bus connection), and Marine World Africa USA in Vallejo. Also provides direct ferry service to Sausalito, Tiburon, and Angel Island.

CalTrain

CalTrain is a commuter rail line that makes 30 stops on the peninsula between San Francisco and San Jose. It departs San Francisco from the terminal at 4th and Townsend streets.

Amtrak

Amtrak is the nation's passenger rail system. There are stations in Oakland, Richmond, and San Jose. In San Francisco, Amtrak buses passengers from the Cal Train Terminal at 4th and Townsend to the Transbay Terminal at First and Howard streets. The buses also take passengers to the Oakland Amtrak station.

Greyhound

Greyhound is the U.S.'s only national bus line. It has depots in major Bay Area cities. It is the only transit system that offers direct service from the Bay Area to the wine country, with stops in Sonoma, Napa, Calistoga, and several other locations.

Intra-County Transit Systems

Alameda County

AC Transit buses serve Oakland, Berkeley, and many other Alameda County towns. They also have service across the Bay Bridge, including a stop at Treasure Island, to San Francisco at the Transbay Terminal.

Contra Costa County

The County Connection, as the Central Contra Costa Transit Authority is popularly known, provides bus service throughout this East Bay county. Bus lines connect with all five BART stations in the county.

Marin County

Golden Gate Transit links Marin and Sonoma counties to San Francisco. In San Francisco buses pick up and deliver passengers primarily in the Financial District.

San Mateo County

SamTrans buses provide service from the San Francisco County line to Palo Alto. In addition, they go to San Francisco's Transbay Terminal, and to the Hayward and Daly City BART stations. They also connect with CalTrain stations and with their transit neighbor to the south, the Santa Clara County Transportation Agency.

Santa Clara County

The SCCTA's bus routes take it to BART and AC Transit stations in Milpitas and Fremont. It too connects with CalTrain depots, and in San Jose it picks up and drops off at the Amtrak and Greyhound stations.

Commercial Group Tours

All of the following offer full or half-day tours by van or bus of San Francisco's major attractions. Many go to Sausalito and Muir Woods and a few go as far as Monterey/Carmel and Yosemite. All addresses are in San Francisco unless otherwise noted.

- Agentours, Inc., 126 West Portal, (415) 661-5200.

- Golden Gate Tours, 870 Market Street, #782, (415) 788-5775.

- Gray Line of San Francisco, Powell and Geary streets, or the Transbay Terminal at First and Mission streets, (415) 558-9400. Gray Line is the biggest tour operator in The City and has the greatest number of tours.

- Great Pacific Tour Company, 518 Octavia Street, (415) 626-4499.

- Motorized Cable Car Tours, Pier 41 at Fisherman's Wharf, (415) 922-2425. As the name suggests, these tours are conducted on cable cars that have been converted to gasoline-powered vehicles.

- Quality Tours & Superior Travel Services, 5003 Palmetto Avenue, #83, Pacifica, (415) 994-5054.

- Super Sightseeing Tours, 1465 Custer Avenue, (415) 550-1717.

- Superior Sightseeing Company, 642 Alvarado Street, #100, (415) 550-1362.

- Tower Tours, 77 Jefferson Street, (415) 434-8687.

Museums

"Laughing Sal" at the Musée Mécanique in San Francisco.

Ansel Adams Center

250 Fourth Street (between Howard and Folsom), San Francisco.

The Ansel Adams Center is the only San Francisco museum devoted exclusively to creative photography. It features not only the work of Ansel Adams but of a wide variety of 19th- and 20th-century photographers. Recent exhibits have showcased work by Elliott Erwitt, Annie Liebovitz, Cindy Sherman, and George Hurrell, among others.

The Center's emphasis is on fine-art photography, but there is a social ethic as well. A recent photo exhibit on AIDS drew one of the museum's biggest crowds and most emotional responses. Some visitors left with tears in their eyes.

Although the Center considers itself a museum, there are no permanent exhibits. Rather, there are fifteen or more exhibitions held yearly in the five galleries. One of the galleries is dedicated to Ansel Adams, and usually features some of the 125 prints he donated to the AAC to get it started.

The Center is operated by The Friends of Photography, a member-supported, privately-funded organization. It was founded in 1967 by Ansel Adams and several other photographers in order to promote photography as an art, and as a reflection of human experience. The gallery started in Carmel but moved to its present location in 1989.

The small but well-stocked bookstore in the lobby carries a broad selection of books on photography and related subjects.

Phone: (415) 495-7000.
Hours: Tuesday - Sunday, 11 a.m. to 6 p.m. Closed Monday.
Admission: Adults $4.00; Students $3.00; Seniors and Youth (12–17) $2.00; Children (under 12) Free.
Parking: There is a city-owned garage with reasonable rates on Mission between Fourth and Fifth streets a block and a half away.
Wheelchair Access: Yes.

Asian Art Museum

In Golden Gate Park, San Francisco.

This museum, which adjoins the de Young Museum, contains the world's largest collection of Asian art outside Asia.

The Chinese jades seen here, spanning some 3,000 years, are some of the finest in existence. Nearby is a roomful of cast bronze objects — cups, wine pourers, bells, axes, and figurines. The Chinese were also adept at ceramics, as is demonstrated by two small Tang dynasty caparisoned horses covered with a special "three color" drip glazing.

From Japan, a must-see exhibit is the grouping of 18th- and 19th-century six-fold screens of landscapes. They shimmer with azure streams, pearly white chrysanthemums, and golden clouds of polychrome. A magnificent samurai's body armor made of silk and lacquered leather will also seize your attention.

As you move into the India section you will likely be struck by how the human figures are rendered in a more sensuous manner: the females are full-figured and voluptuous. Besides images carved in wood and stone, there are beautifully detailed and colorful paintings of rajahs, and scenes of boar hunting.

From the Himalayas and Tibet are artifacts made from human bone. On display are a skull bowl and ewer made of bone and hammered copper. A glass case holds an apron made entirely of human bone beads.

Other countries represented include Thailand, Cambodia, Indonesia, Burma, and Vietnam.

Phone: (415) 668-8921.
Hours: Wednesday - Sunday, 10 a.m. to 5 p.m.; Thursday to 8:45 p.m.
Admission: Adults $5.00; Seniors $3.00; Youth (12–17) $2.00; Under 12, Free. Free admission to all on the first Wednesday of the month.
Parking: Parking is available in front of the California Academy of Sciences across from the museum, or on major throughfares in the park.
Wheelchair Access: Yes.

Behring Auto Museum–Blackhawk

3700 Blackhawk Plaza Circle, Danville.

Walking into the Behring Auto Museum is like visiting a fantasy auto showroom for millionaires. While classical music plays in the background you stroll across polished granite floors past rows of mint-condition, spit-and-polish classic automobiles. After viewing the autos in the permanent collection on the first floor you ascend the massive carpeted dual stairway past the grand piano on the landing to the second floor, where the museum presents changing exhibits of cars from worldwide collections.

The museum focuses on rare and custom-built autos, primarily from the 1920s and 1930s, but it also serves to illustrate the automobile's evolution from a horseless carriage with lanterns as headlights to streamlined sports cars of the 1960s. Vehicles range from a turn-of-the-century Oldsmobile to a clutch of Jazz-Age Mercedes Benzs and Duesenbergs to some 1950s Alfa Romeos that look like prototypes for the Batmobile.

There is also an emphasis on autos owned by celebrities. The permanent collection holds a 1920 Pierce Arrow that belonged to Fatty Arbuckle. Recently on view on the upper floor was a 1926 Isotta Fraschini that was ordered by Rudolph Valentino. It took three years to build; Valentino died just before delivery.

If you tire of all this automotive opulence you can sit for awhile in the oversized black leather chairs that adorn the lobby. The museum adjoins the U.C. Berkeley Museum. If you visit both museums, a dual-admission ticket will save you a dollar off the single museum admission price.

Phone: (510) 736-2277.
Hours: Tuesday - Sunday, 10 a.m. to 5 p.m., Wednesday and Friday until 9 p.m. Open Mondays during the summer.
Admission: Adults $5.00; Seniors and Students $3.00; Children (6 and under) Free.
Parking: Free.
Wheelchair Access: Yes.

Cable Car Barn and Museum

1201 Mason Street (at Washington), San Francisco.

With the possible exception of the Golden Gate Bridge, the cable cars have come to symbolize San Francisco more than any other attraction. The cars, which are confined to three routes in the northeast corner of San Francisco, go up and over some of its steepest hills. Along the way they pass by some of the most colorful and scenic parts of the city.

The Cable Car Barn — which is where the cars go at night — provides a look at their operation and history. From a view deck above the machinery you can watch the cables come winding in and out of the building. Information boards with drawings tell how the system works and how the cars are able to move along city streets as they do.

Among the artifacts on display is a unique item — the first cable car, dating from 1873. The cable car was invented by Andrew Hallidie; this is the very car he rode on its inaugural run. The car survived the 1906 earthquake and fire because it was in Baltimore at the time for an exhibition.

Other items to be seen here are two other antique cable cars dating from 1876. Also on view are a couple of grips. These large pieces of steel with handles on the end are used to grab onto the moving cable below the street.

Before leaving, stop in the sheave room downstairs and look through the glass at the giant wheels and moving cables. This is what is going on under the streets where the cable cars run.

Phone: (415) 474-1887.
Hours: Open daily, April to October, 10 a.m. to 6 p.m.;
November to March, 10 a.m. to 5 p.m.
Admission: Free.
Parking: Finding parking in this neighborhood is difficult.
Why not take a cable car to the museum?
Wheelchair Access: Yes except for the view of the sheave room.

California Academy of Sciences

In the eastern end of Golden Gate Park, San Francisco.

The California Academy of Sciences is one of the largest and best natural history museums in the United States. It's collections, which total over 14 million specimens, chart life from the cosmic dust generated at the beginning of the universe to 20th-century man. Contained within the museum's walls are the Steinhart Aquarium and the Morrison Planetarium.

The main museum consists of several halls. The Wild California Hall houses specimens of California animals and plants in re-creations of their native environments. Among them are a tule marsh with elk, a mountain slope with a grizzly bear and cub, and a "between the tides" scene complete with a sea otter under the water, with air bubbles emanating from its nose. The most appealing exhibit here is the "Farallon Spring," a rock wall set amidst a 10,000-gallon tank filled with sea urchins and fish. A periodic whoosh of water evokes tidal action at the Farallon Islands, a marine and bird sanctuary outside the Golden Gate.

Across the lobby is the African Safari Hall. It shows leopards, monkeys, lions, and other animals in lifesize habitat scenes with painted backdrops. The highlight here is the African Waterhole exhibit with its giraffes, zebras, antelopes, and gazelles. At regular intervals the lights dim, and background animal noises are turned on to create the effect of night on the African savannah.

The Academy's newest exhibit hall is its award-winning "Life Through Time," a long passageway that chronicles the step-by-step evolution of life on earth. Through the use of video, interactive computers, live and stuffed animals, and lifesize models, the exhibit charts the development of plant and animal life from single-celled organisms to mammals. The period of the dinosaurs attracts the most attention; here you will find large dinosaur fossils, footprints, and a full-sized skeletal model of an allosaurus attacking a comptosaurus. Frighteningly real is a tableau of three deinonychuses — velociraptor-like dinosaurs with long, sharp claws and teeth — charging through the forest right at you.

The **Steinhart Aquarium** also has an impressive collection of specimens. Most of these, however, are alive. If you enter from the fountain courtyard you will come straight to "The Swamp." Scattered about the pit below the waterfall you will see alligators, crocodiles, and giant turtles. The small, glass-enclosed cases surrounding this area contain snakes, including some of the dealiest known to man — rattlesnakes, vipers, and cobras to name a few.

Walk west through the hallway to start your tour of the fish tanks. Off to the left you will come to a popular attraction — the seals and dolphins tank. Facing it is the penguin pen, stocked with black-footed or "jackass" penguins. Press the button to listen to them and you'll know why they got their name.

Before leaving the aquarium be sure to see the showpiece "fish roundabout." Walk up the spiral ramp and you will find yourself in the center of a circular, 100,000-gallon fish tank. Swimming among schools of silvery fish are several kinds of sharks, bass, pampano, red snapper — even a few batrays.

In the **Morrison Planetarium** you can sit back in comfortable chairs, look upward at the domed ceiling, and enjoy a journey to the heavens. Daytime shows cover traditional night-sky phenomena; evening presentations beam multicolored laser lights off the ceiling and around the room. The latter shows, which are called Laserium, are heightened by background music ranging from classical to rock, depending on the program. Before entering the planetarium you can get in the mood in the Earth and Space Hall, which has space travel exhibits, including a moon rock.

Phone: (415) 750-7145. For the Morrison Planetarium program and schedules call 750-7127 or 750-7141.
Hours: Open daily 10 a.m. to 5 p.m.; extended to 10 a.m. to 7 p.m. from July 4 through Labor Day. The Morrison Planetarium's Laserium shows (phone 750-7138) are held Thursday through Sunday evenings.
Admission: Adults $7.00; Seniors (65+) $4.00; Youth (12–17) $4.00; Children (6–11) $1.50; under 6, Free. Admission fees for the Morrison Planetarium range from $1.50 to $2.50 for the daytime shows and from $4.50 to $6.50 for the nightime Laserium shows.
Parking: Parking is available either in the concourse area in front of the museum or on Middle Drive East in back of it.
Wheelchair Access: Yes.

Cartoon Art Museum

655 Third Street (between Brannan and Townsend), San Francisco.

The Cartoon Art Museum features changing exhibits of original cartoon art ranging from "Peanuts" to "Batman" to animation work for movies and television. On display are such things as original line drawings, animation "cels," and state-of-the-art computer-generated images.

At any one time the three galleries may display such disparate work as storyboards and cels from Walt Disney's 1937 classic *Snow White and the Seven Dwarfs*, original drawings by Edward Gorey, and examples of Colossal Pictures' work on "Liquid Television" for MTV.

Interesting to see is not only how sketches go to ink drawings to finished cels or color artwork, but also just how mundane the creative process can be. On *Snow White*, for example, one finished pen and ink sketch had the following instructions in the margin: "Inker: From here to H-31 be super careful of inking accurately."

There is a small gift shop at the entrance that sells cartoon-related material including comic books, autographed exhibition catalogs and books, and even original cartoon art.

Phone: (415) 546-9481 or 546-3922.
Hours: Wednesday - Friday, 11 a.m. to 5 p.m.;
Saturday, 10 a.m. to 5 p.m.; Sunday, 1 to 5 p.m.
Admission: Adults $3.00; Seniors and Students $2.00;
Children (under 12) $1.00.
Parking: Look for metered and unmetered spaces on nearby streets.
Wheelchair Access: Yes.

Chinese Historical Society of America Museum

650 Commercial St. (between Montgomery and Kearny), San Francisco.

Located just a few doors up from the Pacific Heritage Museum (see p. 23), this one-room, basement-level museum documents the Chinese experience in America. Most of the artifacts come from the Bay Area, however, and the emphasis is on Chinese life in and around San Francisco.

Despite the lack of space, the many artifacts graphically convey the way life must have been for pioneer Chinese in their adopted home. Among the items on display are a gold miner's rocker, an ancient handmade wheelbarrow, a several-foot-long braided queue, an altar from a Chinese temple, an opium pipe, and an herb shop's wooden sign, whose ideographs translate as "Ginseng, deer antlers, and prepared drugs."

The artifacts are nicely complemented by descriptive text and by enlarged historical photographs, a number of them showing Chinese at work shoveling dirt, sawing lumber, and laying railroad track — just a few of the many jobs Chinese performed in northern California and the West in the 19th century.

Chinese-American accomplishments of the 20th century have not been neglected. There are photos on the wall of the first Chinese woman to vote in a presidential election (in 1912) and of several Chinese-American recipients of the Nobel Prize.

But the Chinese experience is not all one of hard work and achievement. A giant, gaily-decorated dragon's head reminds us that Chinese New Year is one of the most festive of holidays.

Phone: (415) 391-1188.
Hours: Tuesday - Saturday, 12 noon to 4 p.m.
Admission: Free.
Parking: The parking lot under Portsmouth Square a half block to the north is the closest and least expensive.
Wheelchair Access: No.

Coyote Point Museum

Coyote Point Park, San Mateo.

Nestled in a grove of eucalyptus trees near the shore of San Francisco Bay, the Coyote Point Museum houses a multi-level gallery focused on the plant and animal world of the Bay Area. Its aim is to foster an appreciation of the natural world, humanity's place in it, and the impact humans have on the environment.

This well-appointed museum, beautifully furnished floor to ceiling in natural woods, is spread over descending levels; each is meant to replicate on a small scale a different Bay Area environment. The the upper level exhibits cover mountains and forests, the middle level grasslands and chaparral, and at ground level are displays on the baylands and coast. The information is conveyed through dioramas of animals in their habitats, through information boards supplemented by photographs and artwork, and through user-friendly computers.

One exhibit certain to get your attention is the rattlesnake in a lucite box. Step on a sensor on the floor and a rattler—thankfully no longer alive—shakes its coils at you with a menacing hiss.

There are live animals here as well. Outside is the Wildlife Habitat, where you can get a close look at animals native to northern California, such as owls, raccoons, and river otters.

Surrounding the museum is Coyote Point Park. Paved hiking trails wind along the shoreline and provide good views of the bay. The park also offers recreational activities such as swimming, boating, and golf.

Directions: From Hwy. 101 take the Poplar Avenue exit; follow the signs.
Phone: (415) 342-7755.
Hours: Tuesday -Saturday, 10 a.m. to 5 p.m.; Sunday, Noon to 5 p.m.
Museum Admission: Adults $3.00; Seniors (62+) $2.00; Children (6–17) $1.00. Admission to the park costs a separate $4.00 per vehicle.
Parking: Free.
Age Range: All ages.
Wheelchair Access: Yes.

The de Young Memorial Museum

In Golden Gate Park adjoining the Asian Art Museum, San Francisco.

The M. H. de Young Memorial Museum is the premier art museum in San Francisco. Its collections cover art spanning 3,000 years and a diverse array of cultures, ranging from ancient Greece to Africa to Central and South America.

The de Young's strength is its collection of American art — paintings, sculpture, and decorative arts — dating from colonial times to the mid-20th century. A few of the early gems include a silver tankard made by Paul Revere, a Duncan Phyfe sofa, and several fine Gilbert Stuart portraits of prominent Bostonians.

It is in art from the mid-to-late 19th century, particularly landscape and genre paintings, that the de Young really shines. Notable paintings include: Albert Bierstadt's huge canvas *California Spring* and George Caleb Bingham's *Boatmen on the Missouri* Among well known names represented are John Singer Sargent, James McNeill Whistler, and Frederick Remington.

A recent addition is the Art of the Americas gallery, which has over 150 objects made by the indigenous peoples of North, Central, and South America. On view are such things as Alaskan ivory figurines, Mexican earthenware bowls, and Colombian gold pendants. A highlight is a rare onyx Aztec mask.

The de Young also hosts significant temporary exhibitions. Two recent ones were "Teotihuacan: City of the Gods," and "The Mystery of the Dead Sea Scrolls."

Phone: (415) 863-3330.
Hours: Wednesday - Sunday, 10 a.m. to 5 p.m.; Thursday to 8:45 p.m.
Admission: Adults $5.00; Seniors $3.00; Youth (12–17) $2.00; Under 12, Free. Free admission to all on the first Wednesday of the month and the first Saturday from 10 a.m. to 12 Noon. Prices include same-day admission to the Asian Art Museum.
Parking: Free parking is available in front of the California Academy of Sciences across from the museum, or on major park thoroughfares .
Wheelchair Access: Yes.

Fort Mason Center museums

In the northwest corner of Fort Mason, San Francisco.

The Fort Mason Center is home to several small museums based on ethnic themes and artists. Although some have extensive permanent collections, these museums function mainly as art galleries, since they devote most of their space to exhibits that change every few months.

The **San Francisco Craft and Folk Art Museum,** located in Building A, (415) 775-0990, has recently featured such diverse things as classical Chinese furniture, Jewish papercuts, and samples of hand bookbinding. Exhibitions are often accompanied by lectures and demonstrations. The small gift shop is notable for the high quality of the items it stocks, including jewelry, cards, calendars, picture frames, and exotic items such as Phillipine candlesticks, Russian dolls, and Mexican decorative glass.

The **Museo Italo Americano,** in Building C, (415) 776-2200, displays the work of Italian or Italian-American artists. Exhibits change about every two months. Noted children's illustrator Tomie de Paola recently had a one-man show here. Before that a display of Italian-made motorcycles drew large crowds.

Across the hall is the gallery space of the **San Francisco African-American Historical and Cultural Society,** (415) 441-0640. Works here are devoted to artists of African descent. Building D houses the **Mexican Museum,** (415) 441-0404). Although it has a large permanent collection, only a few pieces are on display at any one time. The museum's objective is to promote Latino art and culture covering the entire range from ancient to contemporary.

Access: The automobile entrance is on Buchanan Street at Marina Blvd.
Hours: All the museums are open Wednesday–Sunday, 12 noon to 5 p.m. The Craft and Folk Art Museum is open Tuesday–Sunday, 11 a.m. to 5 p.m.
Admission: Admission fees range from free at the African-American Society to $3.00 at the Mexican Museum.
Parking: Free parking lot.
Wheelchair Access: Yes.

Jewish Museum San Francisco

121 Steuart Street (between Mission and Howard), San Francisco.

In most museums you stroll around and admire the pretty pictures or objects. The Jewish Museum makes you dig deeper. The emphasis is on Jewish art, history, and culture, but the exhibitions explore universal human themes of interest to all.

The museum has no permanent collection; instead it mounts from four to six changing exhibitions per year. Particularly noteworthy is the artistic sensibility and attention to detail given to the installations.

One of the more recent shows featured *Maus*, Pulitzer Prize-winning cartoonist Art Spiegelman's moving evocation of his parents time spent in the Nazi death camp Auschwitz. Spiegelman's cartoon strips of Nazi guards as cats and the Jewish prisoners as mice were laid out inside a simulated wire cage. Nearby was a re-creation of the artist's drawing board complete with his pens and brushes.

Examples of other recent exhibitions are: "A Day in the Warsaw Ghetto," photographs taken by a German soldier in 1941; the "Purim Mask Invitational," which explored the role of masks in different cultures; and "Bridges and Boundaries," which looked at the relationship between African Americans and American Jews in the 20th century.

Many of the exhibitions are accompanied by student workshops for grades K–12. Students absorb the lessons of the shows by wearing masks, for example, or by drawing their own cartoons à la Spiegelman.

Phone: (415) 543-8880.
Hours: Sunday - Wednesday, 11 a.m. to 5 p.m.; Thursday until 7 p.m.
Admission: Adults $3.00; Seniors and Students $1.50;
Children (under 12) Free.
Parking: Take public transit if possible; nearby street and garage parking is expensive.
Wheelchair Access: Yes.

Judah Magnes Museum

2911 Russell Street (between Pine and Claremont), Berkeley.

The Judah Magnes Museum, with an extensive permanent collection and changing exhibitions, helps keep alive Judaism's rich cultural heritage. Named for the first ordained rabbi west of the Mississippi, the museum occupies a beautiful house in a choice area of Berkeley.

The museum's second floor houses its permanent collection. The Holocaust was the central event of Jewish experience in the 20th century. On display are artifacts documenting that terrible time: a concentration camp inmate's shirt and shoes; a yellow Star of David that all Jews were forced to wear; and a torah scroll that was torched by the Germans.

On view elsewhere on this floor are such traditional Jewish artifacts as torah pointers, breastplates, and Passover plates. There also is a grouping of silver and brass hanukkah lamps from all over the world. Some rarely seen items include a collection of antique circumcision knives.

The rooms on the first floor, which have been converted to gallery space complete with track lighting and blond hardwood floors, contain changing exhibitions. Some recent shows have included artifacts, paintings, and engravings depicting shtetl life of East European Jews, photographs of present-day Ethiopian Jews, and paintings by California Jewish artists.

The Judah Magnes Museum is the home of the Western Jewish History Center, which serves as an archive for materials on Jews of the western United States. The museum also houses a separate rare book and manuscript library.

Directions: From Ashby Ave. go north on Pine or Claremont to Russell.
Phone: (510) 849-2710.
Hours: Sunday - Thursday, 10 a.m. to 4 p.m.
Admission: $3.00 donation.
Parking: Free parking on Russell Street for up to two hours.
Wheelchair Access: No.

Marin Museum of the American Indian

2200 Novato Boulevard, Novato.

The name of this museum is a misnomer, since it does not cover all American Indians but focuses exclusively on the Coast Miwok, the indigenuous people of Marin County. Nevertheless, the museum does a fine job of depicting their lives and culture as they existed before the coming of Europeans and Americans.

Particularly good are the exhibits on the techniques and tools used for trapping, fishing, and hunting. Shown, for example, is a realistic decoy such as the Miwok used to lure ducks. There is also a nice display on how arrows and arrowheads were made. Other items include baskets, fish traps, and stone and flint tools.

Most of the objects here are replicas or are from other California tribes, because the influx of the gold-rush hordes from 1849 on destroyed virtually all Miwok artifacts. The representative items on display are complimented by enlarged photos on the walls showing some of the last full-blooded Indians in California.

A free Sunday docent-led tour in the adjacent park is well suited for children, since it ends in the museum's basement where they are encouraged to handle and play with toys and tools of the sort the Miwok made and used. One example is a deer's-head disguise made from an actual head and fur from a deer. A quote from an early European observer describes how very effective this was in allowing Indian hunters to get close enough to the real thing to kill their prey.

Directions: From Highway 101 take the Novato Boulevard exit.
Phone: (415) 897-4064.
Hours: Wednesday - Friday, 10:00 a.m. to 3:00 p.m.; Saturdays and Sundays, 12 noon to 4:00 p.m.
Admission: Free.
Parking: Free lot.
Wheelchair Access: Yes for the basement level only.

Musée Mécanique

In the basement of the Cliff House, 1090 Point Lobos Avenue (at Land's End), San Francisco.

Here's a rare museum — one where you can actually play with the objects themselves. Stocked with antique penny arcade machines the Musée Mécanique affords a chance for youngsters raised on video games to play the arcade games their parents, grandparents, and even great-grandparents played.

There are player pianos that play lively tunes, sports games such as baseball, basketball, and horse racing, and you can see what passed for skin flicks circa 1910 — drop-picture machines with such alluring titles as "See What the Belly Dancer Does On Her Day Off," and "Have A Look In The Sultan's Harem." Most cost a quarter; a few are fifty cents.

Some of the highlights are a 1930s' baseball game, a circus diorama with many moving parts, and Grandma the Fortune Teller, a lifelike head and torso of a gypsy woman who moves her head and looks directly at you with realistic big blue eyes.

On the open-air deck behind the Musée Mécanique is the **Camera Obscura**. A camera obscura operates on the ancient principle that when a small hole of light is allowed into a dark room and captured on a screen it projects a live, moving image of what is going on outside. Inside this darkened box, therefore, you will see with great clarity scenes of people frolicking at Ocean Beach, birds on the nearby rocks, and so forth.

The Camera Obscura is open from 11 a.m. to roughly sunset. There is a nominal admission fee.

Phone: (415) 386-1170.
Hours: Open daily, 10 a.m. to 8 p.m.; open weekdays during the winter from 11 a.m. to 7 p.m.
Admission: Free.
Parking: Plenty of free parking nearby.
Wheelchair Access: Yes. Enter from the south side of the building near the totem pole.

Museum of American Heritage

275 Alma Street (near Everett), Palo Alto.

In an age where we take advanced technological marvels for granted, this attractive museum provides a useful look at the forerunners and earlier models of today's machines. The focus is on household and consumer appliances and business machines from the mid-19th century to the mid-20th century — the period prior to the advent of solid-state electronics.

There are early typewriters, including a music typewriter with musical notes for keys, antique phonographs, the showpiece of which is a wonderful 1916 Edison hand-cranked diamond disc model in a big wooden Chippendale case, and an array of cameras. Among the latter is one straight out of James Bond — a Japanese-made combination camera and cigarette lighter.

Household appliances range from irons which, in the days before electricity, were powered by such things as charcoal, natural gas, and liquid fuel, to blow dryers for hair, which existed as early as 1921—as one clunky-looking model on display proves—to toasters, including the first pop-up toaster, which was invented in 1926. Also on view is the "Toast-O-Lator," a kitchen marvel of the 1930s and 1940s in which a slice of bread is inserted in one end of a chrome toaster and comes out the other end as toast.

Two of the museum's rooms are set up as period settings from the 1920s '30s, and are stocked with original artifacts. One is a kitchen and the other is an office complete with rolltop desk and an old 'desk set' phone.

Recent temporary exhibitions have highlighted such things as cameras, toy trains, and clocks.

Phone: (415) 321-1004.
Hours: Friday, Saturday, and Sunday from 11:00 a.m. to 4 p.m.
Admission: Free.
Parking: There is a free lot on High Street behind the museum.
Wheelchair Access: Yes.

Museum of the City of San Francisco

2801 Leavenworth Street — in The Cannery, 3rd Floor — San Francisco.

This new museum features permanent and changing exhibitions dealing with San Francisco's colorful past. Its main area of emphasis is the earthquake and fire of 1906.

Setting the stage for this famous event are several large, panoramic photos of the burning city and then of the ruins afterward. Copies of some newspapers from the time are displayed, including an Oakland Tribune edition 11 days after the event with the screaming headline: "Starving Dogs Are Devouring Scores of Bodies: Canines Dig Open Graves."

Other 1906 memorabilia include relics salvaged from the ruins, such as scorched china, two pewter sugar bowls fused together, and glass bottles melted into strange shapes.

The Loma Prieta earthquake of 1989 also receives some attention. There are numerous photos of the damage caused—particularly of the collapsed Cypress structure in Oakland, which is where 43 of the 67 victims died.

Among other items to be seen here are a coin-operated piano from the Barbary Coast — pop in a dime, it still plays — and the tin box time capsule from the old City Hall of 1872 and the artifacts that were found inside, including a small bottle of California champagne.

Phone: (415) 928-0289.
Hours: Wednesday - Sunday, 10 a.m. to 4 p.m.
Admission: Free.
Parking: Metered street parking nearby or try The Anchorage Shopping Center garage at 500 Beach Street.
Wheelchair Access: Yes.

Museum of Money of the American West

400 California St. (between Sansome and Montgomery), San Francisco.

This small museum, located in the basement of the Bank of California's main branch, is packed with artifacts illustrative of San Francisco's early days.

From the days of the gold rush there are nuggets from California mines along with a list showing when and where the biggest ones were found. A glass case nearby has gold coins from the fateful year of 1849 and others from the 1850s.

San Francisco in the 1850s could be a dangerous place. The museum provides physical evidence of this in the form of a pair of beautifully detailed Belgian-made dueling pistols. These were used in a famous duel that took place in San Francisco in 1859, in which U.S. Senator David C. Broderick was mortally wounded. A descriptive panel in the same corner tells the story of James King of William, a crusading newspaper editor, who was killed by a man who felt he had been libeled by King's paper.

Another item found here is San Francisco's first municipal bond issue, dated 1851, and signed by John W. Geary, the city's first official mayor. The bond, which paid 10% interest, still has all its coupons attached; the last was paid in May 1871.

A final treasure for history buffs — framed in a glass case — are the original assay pellets that started the great silver rush to Virginia City in the 1860s.

Phone: The museum has no separate phone, but the bank's main number is (415) 765-0400.
Hours: Monday - Thursday, 10 a.m. to 4 p.m.; Friday, 10 a.m. to 5 p.m. Closed bank holidays and weekends.
Admission: Free.
Parking: The nearest, least expensive parking lots are city-owned garages — either the one under Portsmouth Square or the Stockton-Sutter garage.
Wheelchair Access: Yes.

Museum of Russian Culture

2450 Sutter St. (between Divisadero and Broderick sts.), San Francisco.

This out-of-the-way museum is musty and dimly lit, but the homemade exhibits, crafted by Russian emigres to honor their homeland and its culture, give this place a certain charm. The captions are in Russian with only some translated into English, but a bilingual caretaker is present to answer any questions.

The most striking objects are a grouping of armaments dating from the 10th to 15th centuries. On view is an impressive coat of chain mail, a matching shield and helmet inlaid with Arabic designs, a Tartar sword and dagger, and a lethal-looking Russian pole axe. This is very likely the only such place in northern California where you'll be able to see such rare items.

Much of the museum focuses on Imperial Russia (pre–1917) and on the czars and emperors in particular. Several portrait groups show Russia's rulers dating from the year 862 to 1917 when the last czar, Nicholas II, was overthrown by the Soviets. Individual portraits show a variety of bemedaled royalty and grand dukes, all looking very stern and self-confident.

The Russians are proud of their ties to early California: Fort Ross, a Russian outpost on the Sonoma coast, was established in 1812. On view are photos of the reconstructed fort and a scale model of the quaint wooden chapel.

Other items here include a couple of Russian costumes, one from a production of *Boris Godunov*, the other an 18th–19th century Mordovian bride's costume lavishly embroidered with shells and brass planchets stamped with images of leaping deer.

Phone: (415) 921-4082.
Hours: Wednesdays and Saturdays 10:30 a.m. to 2:30 p.m.
Admission: Free.
Parking: Free street parking but avoid the area of the grim public housing projects a block to the southwest.
Wheelchair Access: No.

National Maritime Museum

At the foot of Polk Street adjacent to Aquatic Park, San Francisco.

This streamlined moderne-style building, which appropriately resembles a ship, houses nautical exhibits and artifacts. Its two floors contain an impressive array of historic photographs, models, ship remnants, and sailing gear.

As you enter, the first things you see are a giant beak-head and bow from a four-masted schooner and a ten-ton anchor, meeting like sword points in the center of the room. The anchor is the last remnant of the U.S.S. *Independence,* the first U.S. warship, which was constructed in 1812. Adorning the walls, and equally impressive, are several full–size, colorfully painted ship's figureheads from barks and clipper ships.

Upstairs is an exhibit on the gold rush. On display are period artifacts such as a brass gold-dust scale, a bullet mold, and a rusted six-shot pistol, all of which were uncovered during recent excavations in the financial district — the location of the original shoreline. There are also rare daguerreotypes of the city's waterfront, including the earliest known photo of San Francisco, taken in 1849, showing the cove thick with a forest of ships' masts.

Other exhibits on this floor focus on Cape Horn sailing ships, whaling (San Francisco was once "the whaling capital of the world"), Bay Area ferryboats, and other related subjects.

Be sure to see the Steamship Room, with its exhibit on West Coast steam power. To get there go back down to the main floor and out onto the deck. It's in the circular room at the west end. The highlight here is the collection of large, finely detailed scale models of steamships some of which are over ten feet long.

Phone: (415) 556-2904.
Hours: Open daily, 10 a.m. to 5 p.m.
Admission: Free.
Parking: Metered street parking, and there is a garage under Ghirardelli Square one block away.
Wheelchair Access: Ground floor only.

The Oakland Museum

1000 Oak Street (at 10th), Oakland.

No museum in northern California does exhibits with greater visual appeal than the Oakland Museum.

The museum's focus is California, and it concentrates on the diversity of the state's people, environment, and culture. The permanent collection is housed in three major galleries — Art, History, and Natural Sciences. The museum also hosts various temporary shows, all with a California theme.

The upper level contains the **Art Gallery.** The paintings (and some sculpture) chart the evolution of California art and artists from the Victorian era through the various abstract styles of the 20th century. Particularly noteworthy are the 19th-century landscapes. You can feel the freshness and sense of awe with which the painters approached and captured the magnificence of the land, water, and sky of early California. A large Albert Bierstadt canvas, "Yosemite Valley," shimmers with light.

The **History Gallery,** one level below, has a rich array of memorabilia that illustrate the history of this vibrant and trendsetting state. You will find everything here from Native American baskets to gold-rush-era mining gear (including a complete 1850s assay office) to Hollywood movie equipment.

On the lower level is the **Natural Sciences Gallery**. Extraordinarily realistic exhibits re-create some of the many different environments in California. Full-size tableaux depict sea gulls circling over a beach, bear cubs playing in the woods, and a hawk bringing rabbits to young ones in the nest, to name just a few.

Phone: 24-hour recorded information (510) 834-2413; public information (510) 273-3401.
Hours: Wednesday - Saturday, 10 a.m. to 5 p.m.; Sunday, Noon to 7 p.m.
Admission: Suggested donations: Adults $4.00; Seniors and students $2.00; Children 6 and under, Free. Free to all on Sundays, 4 p.m. to 7 p.m.
Parking: Under the building; the entrances are on Oak and 12th streets.
Wheelchair Access: Yes.

Pacific Heritage Museum

**608 Commercial Street (between Montgomery and Kearny),
San Francisco.**

Located in an alley just steps away from San Francisco's bus-tling financial district, this elegant, little-known museum is never crowded. It primarily features changing exhibits related to Asian and Pacific Basin culture.

A recent display of Chinese antiquities charting the develop-ment of Chinese decorative methods over a 4,000-year period featured some stunningly beautiful bowls, cups, and ceremonial vessels. Another exhibit shed light on the Buddhist monks of Thailand, and was supplemented with monastery artifacts and photographs.

The building itself, constructed in 1877, is historically signifi-cant, in that it originally housed San Francisco's sub-treasury—a sort of mint that stored bullion and served to facilitate transac-tions between the U.S. Government and private individuals. The Bank of Canton of California, which owns the museum and built the office tower that surrounds it, deserves credit for preserving this piece of San Francisco history.

The museum has a permanent exhibit on the Sub-Treasury Building and its history. From the main floor you can look into the vault and see replicas of strong boxes and coin bags. Take the elevator to the basement for a closer look and you'll see the guard walk around the vault, which is complete with mirrors at the corners — a feature designed to prevent ambush.

Phone: (415) 399-1124.
Hours: Monday - Friday, 10:00 a.m. to 4:00 p.m., except holidays.
Admission: Free.
Parking: The closest and least expensive parking garage is located just a block away under Portsmouth Square (entrance on Kearny Street).
Wheelchair Access: Yes.

The Palace of the Legion of Honor

In Lincoln Park near 34th Avenue and Clement Street, San Francisco.

The California Palace of the Legion of Honor is noted for its fine collection of art and sculpture by European artists. Also noteworthy is the museum's setting. Housed in a replica of a similar building in Paris, it sits on a rise in Lincoln Park with a commanding view of the Golden Gate.

The museum was originally designed to showcase only French artists, but it has since broadened its scope. The works range across eight centuries: from medieval and Renaissance art to baroque and roccoco to impressionist and post-impresssionist. Represented are Fra Angelico, Titian, El Greco, Rubens, Rembrandt, Renoir, Degas, Monet, and Cezanne, among others. Highlights include: one of Rembrandt's finest early portraits; Rubens's *Tribute Money;* a grouping of Monet landscapes; and a recent acquisition, a Picasso — *Still Life with Skull, Leeks, and Pitcher.*

Also not to be missed are the Rodin sculptures — the finest such collection outside the Musée Rodin in Paris. The courtyard holds one of the thirteen original casts of *The Thinker.*

The Legion of Honor also houses the collection of the Achenbach Foundation for Graphic Arts. It comprises nearly 100,000 prints and 3,000 drawings, including some by Durer, Gauguin, and Georgia O'Keefe. Because of limited gallery space, only a tiny portion of the collection can be displayed at any one time.

Note: The museum is closed until Fall 1995 for seismic upgrading and other renovation.

Phone: (415) 750-3600.
Hours: Wednesday - Sunday, 10 a.m. to 5 p.m.
Admission: Adults $5.00; Seniors and Youth (12–17) $3.00;
Children under 12, Free. Free admission the first Saturday morning and the first Wednesday of each month.
Parking: Free parking available across from the museum
or along El Camino del Mar just to the north.
Wheelchair Access: Yes.

Phoebe A. Hearst Museum of Anthropology

Kroeber Hall, across from the corner of Bancroft Way and College Avenue on the University of California campus, Berkeley.

The Hearst Museum, with over four million items, ruefully boasts that it has the largest collection with the smallest amount of exhibit space of any museum in the United States.

The museum uses its one main room to feature changing exhibitions. Founded by Phoebe Apperson Hearst in 1901, the museum's core collection came from archeological expeditions that she sponsored to different parts of the globe.

The major strengths of the collection are artifacts from ancient Egypt, pre-colonial and colonial Peru, and from native American tribes in California and other western states. But there are items from all eras of history and from all parts of the globe. For instance, you may find such things as red-and-black figure vessels from ancient Greece, an Egyptian painted tablet from 2500 B.C., Inuit carved soapstone and ivory animal figures from Alaska, ancestor figures from New Guinea, or some of the earliest human tools recovered from Olduvai Gorge in East Africa.

The only permanent exhibit is on Ishi, a Native American, the last of his tribe, who emerged from the wilds of northern California in 1911. On display are some arrows and arrowheads that Ishi made during the remaining few years of his life. You can also don headsets and listen to Ishi chanting one of his tribal songs.

Phone: (510) 643-7648.
Hours: Tuesday - Friday, 10 a.m. to 4:30 p.m.; Saturday and Sunday, Noon to 4:30 p.m. Closed Monday and holidays.
Admission: Adults, $1.50; Seniors, $0.50; Children, $0.25.
Parking: The closest parking garage with reasonable rates is just west of Telegraph Avenue; enter from Durant Avenue or Channing Way.
Wheelchair Access: Yes.

Presidio Museum

Lincoln at Funston streets in the Presidio, San Francisco.

If you are interested in San Francisco history, especially the 1906 earthquake and fire, this museum is a good place to find out more, since the Presidio had a major part in this and other historic San Francisco events.

San Francisco, in fact, was founded at the Presidio in 1776 when the Spanish established a compound where the parade ground is today. Artifacts at the museum from the days of Spanish rule include a pair of leather half-boot Spanish stirrups, an eight-pound cannon ball found on the grounds, and some pottery fragments uncovered during a recent archeological dig.

From 1906, enlarged photos on the walls show the city-wide effects of the quake, the fire, and the aftermath. Among the artifacts on display is a singed wooden dynamite box panel that was found in the ruins. Also of interest is a diorama of Nob Hill depicted as it looked as the flames were approaching.

From the Panama Pacific International Exposition world's fair of 1915 (partially held on the Presidio grounds) are some photographs, souvenir postcards, and medallions. A highlight is a diorama of the fair and its major buildings.

The museum also has exhibits on the Spanish-American War, World War I, and the Coast Artillery and its role in defending San Francisco during World War II, among others. Uniformed mannequins, photographs, and other items supplement the displays.

Also worth a look before leaving the grounds are the two refugee cottages behind the museum. Earthquake victims lived in shacks such as these following the 1906 disaster.

Phone: (415) 921-8193 or 561-4115.
Hours: Wednesday - Sunday, 10 a.m. to 4 p.m.
Admission: Free.
Parking: Free lot across from the museum.
Wheelchair Access: Yes.

Ripley's Believe It or Not! Museum

175 Jefferson Street (between Taylor and Mason), at Fisherman's Wharf, San Francisco.

Robert Ripley was a newspaper cartoonist who travelled the world in the 1920s, '30s and '40s in search of human and natural oddities for his "Believe It or Not" cartoons. This museum documents the strange and unusual things he came across.

Some of things are actual artifacts and some are re-creations. A sample of the things you'll find here: a two-headed calf; a shrunken head and torso of a woman; an acoustic guitar made from a French bidet; and for local interest, an eight-foot-long cable car made from matchsticks. There are also videos of such things as people swallowing razor blades, lighted cigarettes, and other unpleasant objects.

The most interesting thing in the museum, however, is the story of Robert Ripley himself. Film footage transferred to video shows the intrepid Ripley in exotic locales all over the globe. He not only made many of his journeys by car but he also owned a number of top-of-the-line automobiles. Yet he never learned how to drive!

After viewing the video of Ripley's life you can see a few museum-quality antiques and curios Ripley brought back with him — a New Guinea fertility statue, a cloisonné opium pipe, and a crocodile totem.

If you're a little squeamish you may want to avoid looking at the photos near the museum's exit, where there are pictures of people with their bodies impaled by pipes, augurs, and the like.

Phone: (415) 771-6188.
Hours: Open daily, 11 a.m. to 10 p.m., with extended hours on weekends.
Admission: Adults $7.25; Seniors $6.25; Children (5–12) and Students $6.00.
Parking: Try the lot across the street, the Anchorage shopping center garage, or street meters.
Wheelchair Access: Yes.

Rosicrucian Egyptian Museum

Naglee and Park streets, San Jose.

This little-known private museum contains the largest collection of Egyptian, Assyrian, and Babylonian antiquities in the western United States. The Rosicrucians is a quasi-mystical fraternal organization that traces its origins to ancient Egypt — hence the interest in collecting such relics.

Egyptian artifacts make up the bulk of the items on display. Mummies are always an attraction, and the Rosicrucian has a wealth of them. Beyond the usual linen-wrapped priests and aristocrats, there are mummified gazelles, crocodiles, and ibises, as well as the head of a bull. Probably the rarest mummy is that of a baboon. It is strikingly life-like after more than two thousand years.

Other items on display document everyday life in ancient Egypt. There are needles, fish hooks, and a axe, all made of bronze; game board pieces made of glass or glazed pottery; and cosmetic utensils such as mirrors, razors, and perfume vases.

Of almost equal interest because of their rarity, are the Sumerian, Assyrian, and Babylonian artifacts. These mainly consist of cuneiform seals and tablets — small clay pieces covered with wedge-shaped characters that are the earliest form of writing. The rarest of the group is a Babylonian cylinder, a proclamation of King Nebuchadnezzar — one of only four known.

The grounds around the museum house other Rosicrucian buildings, such as a research library and a planetarium, but mainly consist of a park that is open to the public. There are palm trees, magnolias, and large stands of papyrus.

Phone: (408) 947-3635.
Hours: Open daily, 9 a.m. to 5 p.m.
Admission: Adults $6.00; Seniors and students $4.00;
Children (7–15) $3.50; under 7, Free.
Parking: Free lot on Chapman Street, behind the museum.
Wheelchair Access: No.

San Francisco Fire Department Museum

655 Presidio Avenue (between Bush and Pine), San Francisco.

This museum, which is located next to an active firehouse in a residential area, is packed with fire-fighting equipment and regalia from the 19th and 20th centuries. Most of the material comes from or documents San Francisco's own fire department.

The nucleus of the museum are the half dozen fire trucks that occupy most of the floor space. The oldest one is San Francisco's first fire engine, an 1810 hand-pumped contraption that was brought around Cape Horn at the time of the gold rush. Trimmed with a leather fringe and painted in its original blue and yellow colors, it has been lovingly restored to mint condition.

Another gem is the completely restored, beautifully painted and polished 1890s steam-powered fire engine. To see just how much work goes into such a restoration compare it to a similar model on the floor that has not yet been worked on.

In the glass cases that line the walls is a variety of artifacts: old leather fire helmets, badges, uniforms, and historic photos, including portraits of 1870s and 1880s fire companies with solid-looking, mustachioed men staring unsmilingly straight ahead.

In a glass cabinet are relics from the 1906 earthquake and fire. There are historic photos of the fire in progress, postcards showing the devastation afterward, and a great color print depicting the spread of the fire from a bird's-eye view. Tangible items include melted glass bottles and a mass of Indian Head pennies, fused together by the heat, which were found in the ruins.

Phone: (415) 861-8000, ext. 365.
Hours: Thursday - Sunday, 1 p.m. to 4 p.m.
Closed the rest of the week and all holidays.
Admission: Free.
Parking: Residential street parking only.
Wheelchair Access: Yes.

San Francisco Museum of Modern Art

401 Van Ness Avenue (across from City Hall), San Francisco.

The San Francisco Museum of Modern Art has one of the country's premier collections of 20th-century art. Its permanent collection comprises over 15,000 pieces.

There are major works by Georges Braque, Alberto Giacometti, Paul Klee and Pablo Picasso. The SFMOMA is also considered to have one of the world's finest collections of Matisse paintings, including his *Girl with Green Eyes,* and *Woman with the Hat.*

Leading postwar American artists such as Jasper Johns, Willem de Kooning, Sam Francis, Jackson Pollock, Robert Motherwell, Claes Oldenburg, Ellsworth Kelly, and Robert Rauschenberg are represented here as well.

Although the majority of the museum's objects are paintings and sculpture, the museum is expanding its scope and is starting to acquire architectural and design objects, including furniture. But photography is now the fastest growing portion of the collection. The permanent photo collection has prints by Alfred Stieglitz, Ansel Adams, Imogen Cunningham, Edward and Brett Weston, and other 20th-century photographers.

In 1995 the museum will move to a new building at 151 Third Street in the Yerba Buena Gardens Complex. There it will have double its present exhibition gallery space.

Phone: (415) 252-4000.
Hours: Tuesday, Wednesday, and Friday, 10 a.m. to 5 p.m.; Thursday, 10 a.m. to 9 p.m.; Saturday and Sunday, 11 a.m. to 5 p.m.; closed Mondays and holidays.
Admission: Adults $4.00; Seniors and students $2.00; Children under 13, Free. Thursday, 5 to 9 p.m., half-price admission. First Tuesday of each month is free to all.
Parking: There is a parking garage under the Civic Center Plaza.
Wheelchair Access: Yes.

San Francisco Performing Arts Library and Museum

399 Grove Street (between Gough and Franklin), San Francisco.

San Francisco has a rich cultural tradition dating back to the early days of the gold rush. The City boasts the oldest ballet company and the second oldest opera company in the United States. Performers ranging from Edwin Booth and Isadora Duncan to modern-day stars such as Isaac Stern and Luciano Pavarotti have appeared on Bay Area stages.

This small museum's changing exhibitions on music, dance, opera, and theater document the Bay Area's lively-arts heritage. The library and museum house over one million items, including such things as historic lithographs, photos, theater broadsides and programs, press clippings, posters, periodicals, books, even costumes. (Only a tiny portion of these is ever on display.)

The artifacts encompass experimental as well as mainstream performances. The collection also documents the wide ethnic variety of entertainment to be found here, including such things as Chinese opera, Spanish dance, and black music, to name a few.

Some recent exhibitions have included "Treasures of the PALM," a sampler of the museum's finest items, one celebrating the 60th anniversary of the San Francisco Ballet, and one on the theatrical works of Jean Cocteau.

The collection concentrates on artists and works of the San Francisco Bay Area but encompasses national and international performing arts as well.

Phone: (415) 255-4800.
Hours: Tuesday - Friday, 10 a.m. to 5 p.m., Saturday, Noon to 4 p.m.
Admission: Free.
Parking: There is a parking garage across the street or there is metered street parking on Grove and nearby streets.
Wheelchair Access: Yes.

San Jose Historical Museum

1600 Senter Road (between E. Alma and Phelan), San Jose.

An open-air living-history center, the San Jose Historical Museum is a re-creation of a combined San Jose residential and business district, circa 1895.

There are two dozen buildings spread over 25 acres. A handful of them are replicas, but the majority once stood elsewhere in San Jose and were moved here. You are free to wander around on your own, but the only way to access most of the interiors is through docent-led tours, given at regular intervals.

The most prominent of the structures is the 115-foot Electric Light Tower. A tubular steel pyramid adorned with electric lights, it is a half-size replica of a tower that stood in downtown San Jose in the late 1800s.

Other buildings include the Empire Firehouse, the Pacific Hotel, a branch office of the Bank of Italy (which later became the Bank of America), the Dashaway Stables, and O'Brien's Ice Cream and Candy Store. O'Brien's offers old-fashioned candy and ice cream for sale as well as sandwiches and more contemporary fare.

On weekends a historic trolley emerges from the Trolley Barn and gives rides up and down the main street.

Directions: Interstate 280 to the 10th Street exit; go south on 10th; left on E. Alma or Phelan.
Phone: (408) 287-2290.
Hours: Monday - Friday, 10 a.m. to 4:30 p.m.; Saturday and Sunday, 12 Noon to 4:30 p.m.
Admission: Adults $4.00; Seniors (65+) $3.00; Children (6–17) $2.00; under 6, Free.
Parking: $3.00 weekends and holidays.
Wheelchair Access: The grounds are accessible; check with the docents or staff for which buildings are.

San Jose Museum of Art

110 South Market Street (at San Fernando), San Jose.

Lovers of 20th-century contemporary art will find a lot to love at the San Jose Museum of Art.

Until the year 2000 the museum is presenting, in several different exhibitions, selected paintings from the permanent collection of the Whitney Museum of American Art in New York. Because of space limitations, 97 percent of the Whitney's collection is in storage. San Jose Museum of Art goers thus have the chance to view some seldom-seen works by Jackson Pollock, Edward Hopper, Georgia O'Keefe, Andrew Wyeth, and Andy Warhol, among others.

The museum is housed in the former main post office, a handsome 1892 Richardson Romanesque building with a sandstone facade. A much larger addition was constructed behind this building in 1991. Its galleries, with their high ceilings, white walls, and blond wood floors, make the perfect setting for the showing of the Whitney paintings.

Besides the Whitney collection, the San Jose Museum of Art showcases other rotating exhibitions of contemporary art and photography. Some recent shows include "Twelve Bay Area Painters," and "New Photography in Mexico."

The museum also sponsors lectures and a popular series of jazz and classical music concerts.

Phone: (408) 294-2787.
Hours: Tuesday - Sunday, 10 a.m. to 5 p.m.; Thursdays until 8 p.m.
Admission: Adults $2.50; Seniors/Students $1.50; Children under 12, Free. Free admission to all the first Thursday of the month.
Parking: Parking garages abound in the area; the three closest are just east of the museum, behind First and Third streets.
Wheelchair Access: Yes.

San Quentin Prison Museum

On the Marin County shore near the Richmond - San Rafael Bridge.

For a museum that is out of the ordinary it is hard to beat the one at San Quentin Prison. Opened in late 1992, it houses a unique and stupefying array of prison gear and weapons dating from the 1850s to the present.

Here you can see the tools of a prison guard's trade: handcuffs; billy clubs; leg irons, including a ball and chain used before 1880; and an "Oregon boot," a thick steel collar once clamped on convicts' legs to keep them from running away. There are also prison restraints such as a wrist-ratcheted "come along," a steel bracelet used on unruly prisoners until it was outlawed in the 1930s.

A glass case holds a collection of rifles and pistols, including an 1873 Winchester, a Browning .30-caliber machine gun, and the 1927 Thompson sub-machine gun used to quell the 1971 George Jackson escape attempt in which six people were killed.

The museum reveals another side of prison life, mainly using historic photos that show inmates performing in variety shows, playing softball, and marching in the prison band.

Another exhibit sheds light on the little-known fact that San Quentin housed women prisoners until 1934. Mug shots from around the turn of the century show two women staring blankly into the camera from under their Victorian-era bonnets.

Directions: From Highway 101 take the Richmond Bridge exit. Follow Sir Francis Drake Boulevard to Highway 580, then immediately exit at Main Street, which leads to the prison gate.
Phone: (415) 454-8808.
Hours: Open daily, 10 a.m. to 4 p.m., but call ahead since this is subject to the availability of volunteers.
Admission: General admission $2.00; Seniors, students, and children under 12 $1.00. To gain entrance to the museum, which is just inside the gate, you must sign in with the guard.
Parking: There is a free lot to the left of the gate.
Wheelchair Access: Yes.

Tech Museum of Innovation

145 W. San Carlos St. (between Almaden and Market streets), San Jose.

"Hands on" is the operative word for many museums today, but nowhere is it more appropriate than at the Tech Museum of Innovation. High technology can be daunting to some, but here simply by pressing buttons and handling various objects you can more easily gain insight into what Silicon Valley is all about.

Stocked with interactive exhibits, the museum is separated into six areas — Space, Microelectronics, Biotechnology, Robots, Materials, and Bicycle Design. In the Space section, for example, is an exhibit called Mars Explorer. Merely press the computer screen and you'll find yourself hurtling over the surface of the planet Mars. The imagery was generated by a computer using actual photos taken of Mars by the Viking I Explorer in 1976.

Just a few of the other things to be found here include a real-life example of how DNA fingerprinting can confirm familial relationships, a robot that will draw a picture of your face, and a bicycle design you generate yourself on a computer.

Under the "I didn't know that category" you'll learn the origin of silicon, whence Silicon Valley takes its name. A silverish-gray silicon ingot sits next to a sample of the raw materials it is made from — quartzite rocks, wood chips, and coal.

A separate room near the museum's entrance houses a bank of computers loaded with educational software, games, and CD-ROMs, which you are free to play around with.

Phone: (408) 279-7150.
Hours: Tuesday - Sunday, 10 a.m. to 5 p.m. Closed Mondays, except for holidays.
Admission: Adults (19–64) $6.00; Seniors (65+) $4.00; Children (6–18) and Students with I.D. $4.00.
Parking: There are several parking garages nearby. The closest is across the street, beneath the McEnery Convention Center; there are entrances on San Carlos, Almaden, and Market streets.
Wheelchair Access: Yes.

Telephone Pioneer Communications Museum

140 New Montgomery (between Mission and Howard), San Francisco.

As the name implies, this museum charts the invention, development, and evolution of the telephone. We take telephones for granted today, but an early 20th-century advertisement on display here touting the telephone as cheaper and quicker than airplanes, trains, and the U.S. mail, points up just what a revolution in communications the telephone truly was.

The displays and artifacts — some are originals and some are replicas — run chronologically, starting with the telephone's invention in 1876 by Alexander Graham Bell. A photocopy of Bell's patent application shows he modestly called his device an "improvement in telegraphy."

Other items include manually operated switchboards (some of which were in use into the 1970s), telephones of the 19th and 20th centuries including the popular 'desk set' model seen so often in early Hollywood movies. More up-to-date is a full-scale model of Telstar, the first communications satellite, launched in 1963.

One of the more unusual exhibits here is called "Causes of Cable Failure." Shown are telephone cables that have had their protective sheaths ripped open by shotgun blasts, rifle shots, an arrow, squirrel bites, and forest fires. It shows how destructive man and nature can be.

The drawback to this museum is that the gallery space is dimly lit and the exhibits are rather tired looking. There are plans, however, to bring it up-to-date (currently the museum only covers developments up until about 1970).

Phone: (415) 542-0182.
Hours: Monday - Friday, 10 a.m. to 3 p.m.
Admission: Free.
Parking: Metered street parking, or garage at Fourth and Mission streets.
Wheelchair Access: Yes.

Treasure Island Museum

Located on Yerba Buena Island in the middle of San Francisco Bay.

This museum devotes most of its space to exhibits detailing the contributions of the U.S. Navy, Marine Corps, and Coast Guard to the defense of the United States over the past 150 years. The focus is on actions in the Pacific and along the California coast.

Historic photos, ship models, and uniformed mannequins help bring to life the major wars the seagoing branches of the service fought in the Pacific from the early 1800s through Vietnam. Other exhibits cover lesser-known things, such as the Coast Guard's war against "rum runners," who, in the 1920s, attempted to smuggle illegal whiskey into U.S. ports from Canada.

The museum also has a giant Fresnel lighthouse lens dating from 1854 that once guided ships into San Francisco Bay, an exhibit on the development of battleships, and an unusual one on Navajo "codetalkers," who were used in World War II to fool Japanese code breakers, who knew English but not Navajo.

The museum also has artifacts from the Golden Gate International Exposition world's fair of 1939–1940, which was held on Treasure Island. In fact, the six large sculptures flanking the front door are a few of the rare major pieces that have survived.

On display from the fair are black-and-white and color photographs and plenty of souvenir items — programs, ashtrays, drinking glasses, pillows, towels, and other knicknacks. A separate portion of the exhibit is devoted to the famed China Clipper, which berthed in the lagoon at the south side of the island.

Directions: Traveling in either direction on the Bay Bridge, stay in the far left lane. Be prepared to slow to 15 mph as you exit.
Phone: (415) 395-5067.
Hours: Open daily, 10 a.m. to 3:30 p.m. Closed federal holidays.
Admission: Free.
Parking: Just before you reach the main gate, turn right and park in the free lot. To get a museum pass, sign in at the guardhouse.
Wheelchair Access: Yes.

University Art Museum

2626 Bancroft Way (between Bowditch and College), Berkeley.

Housed in a modernistic concrete building just across from the U.C. Berkeley campus, the University Art Museum displays a broad array of paintings, sculpture, and photographs. It features works from its permanent collection — selections are on view year-round — as well as changing exhibitions.

The collection's strength is 20th-century art, particularly postwar abstract painting and sculpture, with works on view by Joan Miro, Willem de Kooning, and Robert Motherwell. Contemporary California art is exemplified by such artists as William Wiley, Elmer Bischoff, and Richard Diebenkorn.

Other periods and styles are also represented. There are landscapes by Albert Bierstadt and Thomas Hill, Impressionist works . by Gauguin and Renoir, and German and Italian paintings dating back to the 15th and 16th centuries. One is surprised to find Emmanuel Leutze's *Washington Rallying the Troops at Monmouth*. This giant canvas, which takes up the better part of one whole wall, is the companion piece to the famous *Washington Crossing the Delaware*, also by Leutze, which hangs in the Metropolitan Museum in New York.

Photography exhibits usually highlight the works of individuals. Represented in recent years have been such photographers as Ansel Adams, Cindy Sherman, and Robert Mapplethorpe.

On the first floor of the museum (on the Durant Avenue side) is the Pacific Film Archive. The PFA screens films daily, showing everything from silent classics to experimental foreign films.

Phone: (510) 642-0808.
Hours: Wednesday - Sunday, 11 a.m. to 5 p.m., Thursdays till 9 p.m. Free admission Thursdays from 11 a.m. to 12 Noon.
Admission: Adults $5.00; Seniors (65+) $4.00; Youth (6–17) $4.00.
Parking: The closest parking garage with reasonable rates is just west of Telegraph Avenue; enter from Durant Avenue or Channing Way.
Wheelchair Access: Yes.

U.C. Berkeley Museum, Blackhawk

3700 Blackhawk Plaza Circle, Danville.

Because of the limited space at the Phoebe A. Hearst Museum of Anthropolgy and the U.C. Museum of Paleontology — both at the U.C. Berkeley campus — some of their artifacts have found a home here. And what are on display are choice specimens.

Particularly noteworthy are some of the Native American artifacts. There is a magnificent 19th-century Kiowa woman's buckskin dress, adorned with elk teeth, tassels of hair, and tin tinklers. Among other Indian items are a Seneca war club and a classic Comanche headdress topped with large bird feathers.

Other artifacts from the anthropology section include a Persian bronze helmet and shield inlaid with gold, a collection of Eskimo masks, and a selection of ancient coins, most of which are in mint condition.

The paleontology section boasts a full skeleton of a smilodon, a saber-toothed cat that was abundant in the San Francisco Bay Area up until 10,000 years ago. There also is a mastodon skull that was found near Rio Vista, and — shades of *Jurassic Park* — several chunks of amber with 25-million-year-old insects preserved in them.

A public information officer at the museum describes the artifacts mentioned above as being "semi-permanent," so you may not see these particular ones during your visit, but whatever is on display will likely be just as enthralling. The museum also reserves several rooms exclusively for temporary exhibitions.

Phone: (510) 736-2277.
Hours: Tuesday - Sunday, 10 a.m. to 5 p.m., Wednesday and Friday until 9 p.m. Open Mondays during the summer.
Admission: Adults $3.00; Students (under 18) and Seniors (65+) $2.00; Children (6 and under), Free.
Parking: Free.
Wheelchair Access: Yes.

Vallejo Naval & Historical Museum

734 Marin Street (at Capitol), Vallejo.

This museum highlights the history of nearby Mare Island, a long-time U.S. naval shipyard. The museum secondarily emphasizes the history of the city of Vallejo.

Mare Island was established as a naval reserve in 1853. David Farragut of "Damn the torpedoes, full speed ahead" fame was its first commandant. A major shipyard for over a century, Mare Island built more than 500 ships before its final one — a nuclear-powered submarine — was launched in 1970.

The museum charts this activity through old photographs, invitations to launches, and other documents. Other artifacts on view include a mid-19th-century Marine cannon of sleek design and a mint-condition officers uniform from the 1850s complete with a cape and cockaded hat.

One unique item found here is an honest-to-God periscope from a World War II submarine. It's mounted on a platform on the top floor with its "eye" above the roofline, so when you look into the viewfinder and swivel around you can get a 360-degree look at the city of Vallejo.

The museum's ground floor houses exhibits on the city of Vallejo and its history. There are photos of old Vallejo landmarks, drawings of the first city hall, and a fine oil portrait of Mariano Vallejo, the Mexican general and landowner for whom the town is named.

Phone: (707) 643-0077.
Hours: Tuesday - Saturday, 10 a.m. to 4:30 p.m.
Admission: Adults $1.50; Seniors (60+) $0.75;
Students (12–17) $0.75; Children under 12, Free.
Parking: Free lot off Capitol Street behind the museum.
Wheelchair Access: Yes.

Wells Fargo History Museum

420 Montgomery (between California and Sacramento), San Francisco.

Located in the lobby of the bank's headquarters, this attractive museum charts Wells Fargo's history from its founding in San Francisco in 1852 as a banking and express concern until the present. Since Wells Fargo and San Francisco virtually grew up together, this serves as a museum of San Francisco history as well.

The showpiece object here is an original Wells Fargo stagecoach in a good state of preservation. Nearby are some authentic strongboxes and an exhibit on legendary stagecoach drivers, many of whom were colorful characters.

Gold, of course, is what put San Francisco on the map. Here you'll find a large wall map of the gold-bearing region of California. Below it are samples of the precious metal from many Sierra rivers and streams. Also on view are tools of the miners' trade — shovels, rockers, and pans.

Upstairs, an exhibit in a glass case on the wall tells the story of the notorious highwayman, Black Bart, who robbed over two dozen stagecoaches from 1875 to 1883. When Wells Fargo detectives finally caught up with him he turned out to be an elderly, mild-mannered San Franciscan named Charles Boles.

Also on this floor are artifacts from significant events in The City's history. San Francisco staged three world fairs between 1894 and 1940; here you'll find photos, postcards, and souvenirs from all of them. There are also relics from the 1906 earthquake and fire, including some items fished from the ruins: blackened china fragments; scorched spoons; and two small cylinders of dimes fused together by the tremendous heat the fire generated.

Phone: (415) 396-2619.
Hours: Monday - Friday, 9 a.m. to 5 p.m. Closed weekends and holidays.
Admission: Free.
Parking: The garage under Portsmouth Square a few blocks to the northwest is your best bet.
Wheelchair Access: Yes.

Western Aerospace Museum

8260 Boeing Way, North Field, Oakland International Airport, Oakland.

Aviation, history, nostalgia, and movie buffs will love this museum. Located in a Quonset hut hangar at the Oakland airport, it is stocked inside and out with vintage airplanes, gear, and memorabilia.

The centerpiece of the collection — hard to miss with its 112-foot wingspan — is the British-built flying boat standing outside the entrance. In production just as World War II was coming to a close, it never saw combat. Instead it was later used to carry civilians on the England to South Africa run; sometimes it served to ferry big-game hunters to various stops along the way.

The plane's later history includes ownership by Howard Hughes and a stint in the Indiana Jones movie *Raiders of the Lost Ark*. Take a tour of the plane's interior if you have the opportunity. It provides a fascinating look at what luxury travel was like in the age of propeller-driven aircraft. A fedora hat marks the seat where Harrison Ford sat during filming of the *Raiders* movie.

Inside the museum are more than a dozen American and foreign aircraft dating from the 1920s, '30s, and '40s. A highlight here is a Lockheed L-10 Electra similar to the one Amelia Earhart flew on her final flight. (She took off not far from where this museum stands.)

Separate rooms off the main floor have exhibits on women in aviation, pioneer black aviators, and on General Jimmy Doolittle and his famous bombing run over Tokyo. There is plenty more to see here — videos, mannequins wearing uniforms, and a flight simulator for training pilots, to name a few.

Phone: (510) 638-7100. Call this number for directions.
Hours: Wednesday - Sunday, 10 a.m. to 4 p.m.
Admission: $3.00 per person; 12 and under, Free.
Parking: Free.
Wheelchair Access: Yes, except for the interior of the flying boat.

Western Railway Museum

Located about 55 miles northeast of San Francisco on Highway 12, halfway between Fairfield and Rio Vista.

Set amidst a vast prairie, seemingly in the middle of nowhere, this five-acre outdoor museum has dozens of old trains and streetcars. You can board many of the cars, some of which are restored. The place is run solely by volunteers — rail aficionados all.

The car barn at the back of the lot holds most of the noteworthy specimens. Here you will find a classic red caboose built in 1899, complete with an iron potbellied stove, San Francisco Municipal Railway cars that were in use from the 1920s to the 1970s, and some unusual cars such as the open-air "boat car" used to transport swimmers to the beach at Blackpool, England. A rare gem, still in need of restoration, is an 1888 New York City open-platform railway coach.

The museum also provides the opportunity to ride some antique streetcars. Short trips are given at regular intervals. Of special interest are the car's original advertising placards.

The best time to visit the museum is between mid-March and Mothers Day weekend in May, when you can take a real train ride. The Spring Wildflower Prairie Train Excursion is an hour and a half ride through one of the last unplowed patches of prairie in California. At this time of the year the green native bunch grasses are stippled with bright purple or gold wildflowers. You may see herds of sheep and cattle and an occasional startled jackrabbit.

Directions: From Highway 80 take the Highway 12 exit heading east. It's 13 miles to the museum, which is on the south side of the highway.
Phone: (707) 374-2978.
Hours: Open Saturdays, Sundays, and Holidays, year round.
Admission: Adults (13+) $5.00; Children (4–12) $2.00; Families $15.00. The Wildflower Spring Excursion train costs an additional $7.00 per person for coach class; first class is $25.00 per person.
Parking: Free lot.
Wheelchair Access: Partial. Assistance is needed to board the train and streetcar rides.

Landmarks

The George Patterson House—a Victorian ranch house
at Ardenwood Historic Farm in Fremont.

Alvarado Adobe

1 Alvarado Square (at Church Lane), San Pablo.

The Alvarado Adobe is a reconstruction of a Mexican-era adobe home that stood on this site from 1843 to 1954. The adobe, which had been demolished in the name of progress, was rebuilt in 1978 using historic photos and the original plans.

It is named for Juan Bautista Alvarado, the first Mexican governor of California (1836–1842), who lived here with his family from 1848 until his death in 1882. Alvarado played a bit part in San Francisco's history, for in 1839 it was he who ordered the survey that laid out the first streets in Yerba Buena (as San Francisco was then known).

The adobe's living room has been furnished to resemble how it looked in the 1860s. The Victorian sitting chairs, dining table, and upright piano are donated period pieces. The fireplace andirons, however, are original to the house, as most likely are several family portraits on the walls in beautiful gilt frames.

The bedroom is re-created as it might have looked in the 1840s. Note the plain fourposter bed, the small altar in the corner, and the charcoal-burning brazier on the floor — despite the two-foot thick walls, adobe interiors were cold during the winter.

A short distance away from the Adobe is the **Blume House**, a 1905 cattle-ranch farmhouse. It once stood where the Hilltop shopping center now is, and was moved here in the 1970s. Its interior has been re-created to a 1910s and 1920s look.

Directions: In the East Bay take I-80 to the San Pablo exit, go west on San Pablo Avenue to Church Lane.
Phone: (510) 215-3080 or 3092.
Hours: Open only the third Sunday each month from Noon to 4 p.m.
Admission: Free.
Parking: Free parking in the Civic Center lot just west of Church Lane.
Wheelchair Access: Yes for the Adobe, no for the Blume House.

The Bay Bridge

The 8.4-mile-long Bay Bridge extends from the Alameda shore to (and through) Yerba Buena Island, and feeds into San Francisco in the Rincon Hill area south of Market Street.

The Bay Bridge, or the San Francisco - Oakland Bay Bridge as it is officially known, has always existed in the shadow of its celebrated sister and Bay Area neighbor, the Golden Gate Bridge. In fact, when visitors to San Francisco were asked in a 1980s poll to name prominent landmarks, fifty percent listed the Golden Gate Bridge but only one percent cited the Bay Bridge. The Bay Bridge's recognition level has surely gone up in the wake of the 1989 earthquake. During that tremor a section of the bridge's upper deck collapsed onto the lower deck. Video footage of a motorist plunging to her death into the broken section was broadcast into every home.

The bridge, when it opened to traffic on November 12, 1936, after three and a half years of construction, was the longest in the world. It no longer holds the title as the world's longest bridge, but it still boasts the largest diameter vehicular tunnel.

Until 1958 the lower deck of the bridge was used for trucks and an interurban train line, and the upper deck carried two-way automobile traffic. Since then the bridge has had its current setup, which is five lanes of auto traffic eastbound on the lower deck and five lanes westbound on the upper.

There are numerous places in San Francisco and around the bay that afford good views of the Bay Bridge, but the best way to appreciate this under-rated bridge is to drive it, preferably late at night when traffic is minimal. Driving westbound on the upper deck affords the additional advantage of a stunning view of the lights of downtown San Francisco.

Admission: There is a toll of $1.00 per vehicle westbound into San Francisco. The Bay Bridge has no pedestrian access.

Camron-Stanford House

1418 Lakeside Drive (on Lake Merritt), Oakland.

The Camron-Stanford House is the last survivor of what was once a cluster of Victorian mansions on the shores of Lake Merritt and in the surrounding neighborhood. It was built in 1876, and was a private residence until the City of Oakland purchased it in 1907.

It served as Oakland's public museum from 1910 until 1967, when the new Oakland Museum opened a few blocks away. Scheduled for demolition, it was saved by a group of public-spirited citizens, and was then partially restored.

The highlight is a re-creation of a Victorian home's interior circa 1880. On the main floor the hallway, the front parlor, the family room, and the art gallery have been furnished with Victorian era settees and chairs, statuary, paintings, and bric-a-brac. The front parlor contains an elaborate carved marble fireplace. Few of the pieces are original to the house; most are period antiques donated by interested parties.

On the ground floor (where the entrance is) one room features photos of and a few artifacts from the Camron-Stanford house's museum days. Another room showcases the post-1967 restoration efforts. A third room houses a small gift shop and serves as an auditorium for several well-crafted multi-media slide shows.

The Camron-Stanford home offers docent-led guided tours only. There are no set times; tours are given frequently.

Phone: (510) 836-1976.
Hours: Wednesdays, 11 a.m. to 4 p.m.; Sundays 1 p.m. to 5 p.m.
Admission: Adults, $2.00; Seniors, $1.00; Children (under 12), Free.
Parking: Metered street parking is available nearby.
Wheelchair Access: Ground floor only.

Coit Tower

Coit Tower rises from the summit of Telegraph Hill in San Francisco.

In a city of superb views, the ones from Coit Tower may be the best. From the cul-de-sac parking lot you enjoy sweeping vistas of San Francisco Bay from the Golden Gate Bridge to the Bay Bridge. The top of Coit Tower itself provides panoramic views in every direction: Russian Hill and the north waterfront to the west; Angel Island and Marin County to the north; Treasure Island and the East Bay to the east; and downtown San Francisco and Nob Hill to the south.

Coit Tower is the result of a bequest made by a local eccentric, Lillie Hitchcock Coit, who, when she died in 1929 at the age of 86, left part of her fortune to help beautify the city she loved. This "simple fluted shaft," as its architect Henry Howard called it, was the result. The tower, a combination of classicism and Art Deco, is made of reinforced concrete. It was constructed in 1933 at the height of the Great Depression.

The ground floor is graced by fresco-pinted murals depicting life in California and San Francisco. There was an outcry when the murals were unveiled in June 1934. Done in a style known as "Social Realism," the frescoes depict glum, unsmiling Californians at work in the fields, in factories, and in offices. Several of the panels have a strongly political cast to them, exhibiting a strong sympathy for socialism and communism. The murals generated such controversy that Coit Tower's public opening was delayed for four months.

Directions: The approach by auto or bus is from Lombard Street.
Hours: Open daily 10 a.m. to 7 p.m.
Admission: Free for the ground floor murals; to take the elevator to the top the charges are: Adults $3.00; Seniors (64+) $2.00; Children (6–12) $1.00.
Parking: Free, but there is a 30-minute limit for the 34 spaces on the circle in front of the tower.
Wheelchair Access: No.

The Columbarium

One Loraine Court (one block south of Geary Boulevard between Arguello and Stanyan), San Francisco.

Tucked away in a residential portion of the Richmond District is a little known gem of a building — the Columbarium. A minor masterpiece of cemetery architecture, this Pantheon-like structure serves as a repository for the cremated remains or ashes of more than 10,000 San Franciscans.

It was built in 1898 and was the centerpiece of the 1865 Odd Fellows Cemetery which eventually covered 37½ acres. Today, after the pressures of a developing city caused the disinterment of the cemetery's 26,000 bodies in the early 1930s, only the Columbarium building remains, occupying three acres.

The interior is surprisingly light and airy. This is primarily due to several factors: the primarily white mosaic tile floors done by Portuguese artisans; the art glass dome, which suffuses the interior with light; and the beautiful stained-glass windows, many of which are the equal of those found in major cathedrals.

As you wander through the four tiers, which contain more than 7,000 niches, you can look at the names, dates, and sometimes pictures of the deceased. About half of the niches are sealed with bronze plates; the rest are covered with glass, allowing you to view the urn and any special object enclosed. Urns range from traditional bronze canisters to more elaborate marble, onyx, or porcelain. Some are shaped like flower vases, pitchers, or books. If you are familiar with San Francisco history you will come across notable names associated with its past: Edward Robeson Taylor, a former mayor; Gabriel Moulin, the photographer; John Hittell, the historian; the Hotaling family.

Phone: (415) 221-1838.
Hours: Open daily 10 a.m. to 1 p.m.; guided tours every Saturday.
Admission: Free.
Parking: Free lot adjacent to the building.
Wheelchair Access: No.

Conservatory of Flowers

**Off John F. Kennedy Drive at the eastern end of Golden Gate Park,
San Francisco.**

The Conservatory of Flowers is the grandest Victorian structure in San Francisco, and is the oldest building in Golden Gate
Park. It houses a wide variety of plants and flowers.

Erected in 1879, the structure was imported from Dublin, Ire-
land and is modeled after one in Kew Gardens, London. It is made
entirely of wood, with the exception of its iron columns. The
building came through the 1906 earthquake virtually unscathed,
suffering only a few shattered panes of glass.

Inside, one is reminded of *The Little Shop of Horrors*. The first
things you see are giant leaves the size of elephant ears from a
West Indian xanthosoma plant. Just beyond this is a towering
philodendron from Brazil, which was planted in 1884. A glass case
full of orchids in this room provides the interesting information
that orchids, with over 30,000 species, represent the largest family
of plants in the world.

The east wing houses a cluster of cycads and zamiads, two of
the few plant species that remain from the time of the dinosaurs.
Now endangered, they are found only in parts of Australia, Africa, and tropical America. Beyond these are two ponds covered
with lily pads and stocked with goldfish.

The west wing is mainly devoted to changing seasonal blooms.
At the beginning of the summer the Conservatory's exterior is
whitewashed to protect the plants from sunlight.

Phone: (415) 666-7017.
Hours: Open Memorial Day to Labor Day, 9 a.m. to 6 p.m.; the rest
of the year, 9 a.m. to 5 p.m.
Admission: Adults $1.50; over 65 $0.75; Children (6–11) $0.75;
under 6, Free.
Parking: Free parking is available throughout the park.
Wheelchair Access: Yes.

Dunsmuir House and Gardens

2960 Peralta Oaks Court, Oakland.

The Dunsmuir House, with its classic Colonial Revival facade and its broad, sloping lawns, has been the setting over the years for a number of movies, including *Burnt Offerings* and *So I Married An Axe Murderer.*

This 37-room mansion was built in 1899 by Alexander Dunsmuir, son of a wealthy coal baron, as a wedding present for his new bride. Dunsmuir never got to live in his new house — he died on his honeymoon. Several years after Mrs. Dunsmuir's death, in 1901, the house was purchased by I. W. Hellman, the president of Wells Fargo Bank.

Tours of the mansion are given by docents wearing period costume. Some of the interior's highlights are the beautiful inlaid parquet floors and the Tiffany-style dome skylight, made of 7,000 pieces of glass. Only a few furnishings that belonged either to the Dunsmuirs or the Hellmans remain. The rest were donated or are on loan from the Oakland Museum.

Some of the estate's original outbuildings still stand, including the pool and bath house, the milk barn, the carriage house, and the stables. If the grounds and the landscaping look familiar it's because John McLaren, the longtime superintendent of Golden Gate Park, assisted in designing them.

Directions: From Interstate 580 coming from San Francisco take the 106th Avenue exit; from Hayward take the Foothill MacArthur exit. Turn under the freeway and follow the signs.
Phone: (510) 562-3232.
Hours: Mansion tours are given from April to September, Wednesdays at 12 p.m. and 1 p.m. and the 1st and 3rd Sundays at 12 p.m., 1 p.m., and 2 p.m. The estate grounds are open for longer hours and during other days of the week. Call for information.
Admission: Adults $4.00; Seniors and Juniors (6–13) $3.00; under 6, Free.
Parking: Free parking on the street outside the gate.
Wheelchair Access: Yes for the grounds and the first floor of the mansion.

The Ferry Building

At the foot of Market Street on the Embarcadero, San Francisco.

The Ferry Building was San Francisco's most notable land-mark before the erection of the Golden Gate Bridge in 1937. It was constructed in the mid-1890s and dedicated in July 1898. The architect was A. Page Brown, the designer of City Hall, who modeled the tower after the campanile of Seville's cathedral.

This was the main terminal for the cross-bay ferries that deliv-ered commuters to San Francisco every morning and took them home again every night. By the late 1920s, 50 million people a year, using up to 170 different ferry boats, passed through the Ferry Building's portals, making it the world's second busiest transit hub — second only to London's Charing Cross Station.

The building of the Bay Bridge and the Golden Gate Bridge in the 1930s led to the decline of ferries. The last regularly scheduled commuter ferry run on San Francisco Bay occurred on July 30, 1958. It signaled the end of a bay transportation system that had continued uninterrupted since the days of the gold rush.

In 1975, limited commuter ferry service resumed on the bay in the form of sleek, high-powered diesel boats carrying passengers between Marin County and San Francisco. Service was sub-sequently added to Alameda, Oakland, and Vallejo. Today 1.7 million people annually board the ferries at their docks just be-hind and to the north of the Ferry Building.

The building itself — now dwarfed by the highrises of the downtown business district — survived the 1906 earthquake and the Loma Prieta Quake in 1989. Both times, the clock in the tower stopped at the precise moment of the quake.

Hours: The building itself is open weekdays during regular business hours. The ferries run seven days a week with varying schedules.
Admission: Fees to ride the ferries vary depending on destination.
Parking: There are metered parking spaces along the Embarcadero.
Wheelchair Access: Yes.

Filoli

Cañada Road (near Edgewood), Woodside.

This magnificent Georgian-style country house, set on 654 acres, was built between 1915 and 1917 for William Bourn, owner of the San Francisco water and gas companies and heir to one of the richest gold mines in California. The unusual name Filoli comes from combining the first two letters of "Fight, love, live," from Bourn's credo "Fight for a just cause, love your fellow man, live a good life."

If the sumptuous interior with its Carrara marble fireplaces and Italian Renaissance patterned wallpaper looks familiar, it's because it has been the setting for the movies *Heaven Can Wait, The Joy Luck Club,* and the TV show "Dynasty." Some of the furnishings and fixtures, particularly in the kitchen, are original, but others are on loan from the Fine Arts Museums of San Francisco.

As beautiful as the house is, it is the 16 acres of formal gardens in back of the house that make Filoli a special place. Here amidst neatly trimmed green lawns are 20,000 plantings of many varieties — Irish yews, copper beeches, Coast Live Oaks, Mandarin orange trees, camellias, dogwoods, wisteria vines, and roses, to name a few. An outdoor swimming pool, added by a later owner, further enhances the grounds.

The Filoli mansion will be closed in 1995 for seismic repairs and strenghtening. The gardens will remain open, and a new visitor center will be added while the main house is closed.

Directions: From Highway 280 take the Edgewood Road exit west; turn right on Cañada.
Phone: (415) 364-2880.
Hours: Open from mid-February until early November. Docent-led tours, for which reservations are required, are held Tuesday - Thursday, and Saturday. Self-guided tours are usually allowed on Fridays, and the first Saturday and second Sunday of the month.
Admission: Adults $8.00; Children (2–12) $4.00.
Parking: Free lot.
Wheelchair Access: Yes for the house, only partial access to the garden.

Fort Point

In the Presidio, at the end of Marine Drive, underneath the south end of the Golden Gate Bridge.

This large fort, situated at the entrance to the bay, is unique to the Bay Area, and indeed to the western U.S. — it is the only brick fort west of the Mississippi River.

It was constructed between 1853 and 1861. Although it became operational just as the Civil War began, it never came under attack, and in fact its 120 cannon never fired a shot in anger.

Today, although the cannon have been removed and the case-mates are empty, the fort still looks much as it did during the 19th century. The period flavor is enhanced by park rangers dressed in Civil-War-era uniforms.

The four-story fort has a variety of exhibits and artifacts. The ground floor courtyard contains various armaments. These are centered around a giant 10-inch Rodman gun, a prime example of the guns in place at the fort during its early years.

The second and third floors originally housed the officers and enlisted men. Their living quarters have been partially re-created, but mainly the space has been given over to exhibits on the history of women and blacks in the military.

From the fourth floor, or roof, there are fine views of the bay and the Golden Gate Bridge.

Phone: (415) 556-1693.
Hours: Wednesday - Sunday, 10 a.m. to 5 p.m. Park ranger-led tours and other interpretive programs are given at regular intervals.
Admission: Free.
Parking: There is a free lot outside the entrance.
Wheelchair Access: Ground floor only.

Golden Gate Bridge

The Golden Gate Bridge spans the entrance to San Francisco Bay. It extends from the Presidio in San Francisco to the southern tip of Marin County.

The Golden Gate Bridge is said to be the most photographed man-made structure in the world. It is easy to see why. Its dramatic setting combined with its majestic yet subtle Art Deco design make it a structure for the ages.

An engineering marvel as well as an artistic triumph, it is a prime example of a rare perfect marriage of art and science. A landmark since its completion in 1937, it has become such a symbol of San Francisco that it is hard to imagine The City without it.

The Golden Gate Bridge was named neither for the gold rush nor for its color — which is not gold. It's "international orange," which is more of a rust red. The Golden Gate was named by Army officer and explorer John C. Fremont in 1848 because it suggested to him the form and advantages of the harbor at Constantinople, known as the Golden Horn.

There are several vantage points providing picture-postcard views of the bridge and the surrounding scenery. On the San Francisco side, the most popular viewpoint is at the south end of the bridge near the pedestrian entrance. On the Marin side, the Vista Point turnoff affords sweeping views of the bay and downtown San Francisco. An even more dramatic panorama — of the bridge, the bay, and San Francisco — can be had from along Conzelman Road in the Marin headlands (take the Alexander Avenue exit and cross under the freeway).

Admission: Pedestrians, bicyclists, and northbound vehicles cross free of charge. Southbound automobiles pay $3.00 per vehicle.
Parking: There is a metered parking lot just to the east of the toll plaza (if you're headed north on Doyle Drive stay in the far right lane and exit just before the toll booths).
Wheelchair Access: Yes.

Haas-Lilienthal House

2007 Franklin Street (between Washington and Jackson), San Francisco.

This 24-room, 6½ bath house was constructed in 1886 by William Haas, a Bavarian immigrant who established a successful wholesale grocery business in San Francisco. It is one of the very few 19th-century Bay Area houses open to the public that still has all of its original furnishings.

Architecturally, the house is referred to as "early Queen Anne," because it was one of the first Victorians in the city to use a distinguishing feature of that style — a rounded corner tower. (The tower is strictly decorative; the window in it is eight feet off the floor.) But the house incorporates more elements of the earlier Stick style — with its characteristic rectangular bay windows and "stick" ornamentation — that was popular in the 1880s.

The house's furnishings date from the late 1800s to the 1920s. Even so, it still has a Victorian aura of decorum and propriety, with high ceilings, heavy drapes, and pocket doors between the main rooms.

Guided tours take you outside for a look at the exterior and then inside through the main and second floors. A highlight is the main bathroom upstairs adjoining the master bedroom. Note the bidet, the gas jet for heating hair-curling irons, and the Gothic-looking shower fixture with a separate dial for shampoo.

Phone: (415) 441-3004.
Hours: Sunday, 11 a.m. to 4:30 p.m.; Wednesday, Noon to 3:30 p.m. The last docent-led tour starts about 45 minutes before closing.
Admission: Adults $5.00; Seniors (65+) $3.00; Children (12 and under) $3.00.
Parking: Free parking on neighboring streets but watch for posted time limits.
Wheelchair Access: No.

John Muir National Historic Site

4202 Alhambra Avenue (just off Highway 4), Martinez.

Sitting atop a small hill in Martinez is the 17-room Victorian home where the renowned conservationist John Muir lived from 1890 until his death in 1914. Muir, more than anyone else of his time, pushed for the preservation of wilderness areas and the establishment of national parks. When not tramping the wilderness, Muir spent his days here with his wife and two daughters.

The house is open for self-guided tours. Muir's study, where he wrote many of his books and articles, is on the second floor. The desk and chair are the originals but most of the house's other furnishings are period pieces. Muir's untidy work habits are re-created; the floor is strewn with papers and open books.

The grounds surrounding the house during Muir's time — and today as well — constitute a functioning orchard. As you leave the house you can follow the "Orchard Trail," which will take you past a variety of fruit-bearing trees — peach, cherry, pear, apricot, and orange among others. At the end of the paved road is the 1849 Martinez Adobe, home of the area's original Mexican land grantee.

If you have time, the visitor center (where you enter) shows a 30-minute movie six times daily about John Muir and his times. It's a good introduction to the life and work of this remarkable man.

Phone: (510) 228-8860.
Hours: Wednesday - Sunday, 10 a.m. to 4:30 p.m.
Admission: Adults (17–61) $2.00; Seniors and under 17, Free.
Parking: Free.
Wheelchair Access: Yes for the Orchard Trail and the first floor of the house only.

Lathrop House

627 Hamilton Street (at Marshall), Redwood City.

Amidst a phalanx of modern highrise county government buildings in Redwood City sits an oddity — a quaint Victorian house of "Steamboat Gothic" design, built in 1863.

Its presence is explained by the fact that it was once the home of Benjamin Lathrop, San Mateo County's first clerk, recorder, and assessor. The house managed to avoid the wrecker's ball as government buildings grew up around it.

Today the house serves as a museum and cultural resource for the local community. It has been restored, as nearly as possible, to how it looked in the 1860s. Only a few furnishings and a couple of landscape paintings are original to Lathrop's time; the rest are donated period pieces.

Lathrop's office on the first floor is the most striking of the rooms in terms of re-creating an earlier era. A roll-top desk piled with antique assessor's logbooks and engravings of President Lincoln on the walls evokes the 1860s.

Upstairs, in the master bedroom, a couple of highlights are an 1860 hardwood cradle in perfect working order, and the sponge-bath bathtub made of metal with a leather cover. Also worthy of note is the fine collection of 19th-century dresses on mannequins in the dressing room adjoining the bedroom.

Phone: (415) 365-5564.
Hours: Tuesday - Friday, 11 a.m. to 3 p.m.
Admission: Free.
Parking: One free hour in the city lot one block to the east.
Wheelchair Access: Not yet.

Los Altos History House

51 South San Antonio Road (at the Los Altos Civic Center), Los Altos.

This 1905 Craftsman-style farmhouse has been restored and preserved as an example of the Santa Clara Valley's farming heritage. Now surrounded by the Los Altos Civic Center complex, this small farmhouse was once the focal point of a 10-acre apricot orchard.

Nostalgia buffs will especially enjoy the house's interior, which vividly re-creates the 1930s. The front parlor has comfy, overstuffed couches with crisp, white antimacassars pinned to the armrests. In the corner, an old-time freestanding wooden radio broadcasts FDR's fireside chats, episodes of "The Green Hornet," and the latest news, with Adolf Hitler issuing threats. Combine all this with an original copy of the Palo Alto Times from 1933 resting on an end table, and you almost feel as if you are on the set of a George S. Kaufman play.

Other rooms are equally evocative: the kitchen with its milk bottles and Ball canning jars; the master bedroom with a 1930s issue of Sunset Magazine on the nightstand; and the compact office with its antique typewriter and adding machine.

Out in the backyard, information boards posted in front of various equipment explain the process of gathering, cutting, and drying apricots. Nearby is the water-tank house with a first floor cot for an itinerant worker.

Also nearby is an unusual structure — a deluxe three-seat outhouse that could simultaneously accommodate two adults and one child.

Phone: (415) 948-9427.
Hours: Wednesday, 1 - 5 p.m.; Saturday, Noon - 4 p.m.
Admission: Free.
Parking: Free parking in the Civic Center lot.
Wheelchair Access: Yes.

Luther Burbank Home and Gardens

Santa Rosa Avenue at Sonoma Avenue, Santa Rosa.

Luther Burbank was a horticultural genius known as the "Plant Wizard." Through his plant breeding experiments he created more than 800 new varieties of fruits, flowers, vegetables — even a few trees.

He had an uncanny knack of looking at a plant and knowing what characteristics could be bred into it. A local tavern owner once bet Burbank that he could not create a white blackberry. The tavern owner lost his bet.

The home and gardens where Luther Burbank worked is a National Historic Landmark and is open to the public. Tours start in what was once the carriage house. Both here and in the house are artifacts and memorabilia dating from Burbank's arrival in Santa Rosa in 1875 to his death in 1926.

Burbank's achievements brought him fame. He was visited by the leading celebrities of his day. Photos on the walls show him with Jack London, Helen Keller, Henry Ford, and Thomas Edison. A guest book in a glass case is open to the page with the signatures of the latter two.

Before or after the house tour you can stroll the beautiful gardens surrounding the property. What you will find growing varies by the season, but all the plants are labeled by stakes driven into the ground in front of them.

Phone: (707) 524-5445.
Hours: Open April through October, Wednesday - Sunday, 10 a.m. to 3:30 p.m.
Admission: The house tour is $2.00 per person; 12 and under, Free. The gardens are free of charge.
Parking: Metered street parking available nearby.
Wheelchair Access: Yes.

Mission Dolores

Sixteenth and Dolores streets, San Francisco.

Mission Dolores is the oldest building in San Francisco — a proud survivor of the days when Spain ruled California. The chapel, which is the only building remaining from a number of buildings that once were part of the mission, was constructed between 1788 and 1791. A visit to it and to the adjoining cemetery provides a rare glimpse into San Francisco's earliest days.

Stepping inside the church is like stepping back into the past. Removed from city noise and bustle, the cool, quiet interior evokes the time of nearly two centuries ago. The roof still has the original timbers, which at one time were fastened together with wooden manzanita pegs and rawhide thongs. The altar, with its striking carved wood figures of priests, soldiers, and holy figures, was brought to the church from Mexico in the early 1800s.

There is a small museum behind the church where relics from the mission's early days are on display. Among the items are the church's first baptismal register, started in 1776, and sacred artifacts donated by Father Junipero Serra, founder of the California missions.

Beyond the museum is the oldest cemetery in San Francisco. The headstones reflect the truly international character of the San Francisco that was spawned by the gold rush. Beside the tombstones of early Mexican governors of California and San Francisco alcaldes (mayors) are ones marking the graves of early Irish, French, Italian, English, and Chilean residents.

Phone: (415) 621-8203.
Hours: Open daily during the summer, 9:00 a.m. to 4:30 p.m.; during the winter, 9 a.m. to 4 p.m. Restricted visiting hours on religious and major holidays. Closed Thanksgiving and Christmas.
Admission: $1.00 donation.
Parking: There is no parking lot at the church; try Dolores or nearby streets for parking spaces.
Wheelchair Access: Yes. Ask at the front entrance to gain access.

Mission San Jose

43300 Mission Boulevard (one half mile south of I-680), Fremont.

Mission San Jose is the third of four missions founded by the Spanish in the San Francisco Bay Area. It was established in 1797 when a small chapel with a thatch roof was built a short distance from the present mission. At its peak in the early 1830s the mission was a self-sustaining compound of soldiers, artisans, and Ohlone Indians, under the direction of one or two padres.

Of the mission's first permanent adobe buildings, which were constructed in 1809, only the rectory survives. It now houses a museum containing artifacts that document the mission's history.

The museum's rooms are organized chronologically. You start with the Native Americans and pass through into succeeding rooms, each of which charts another aspect of the mission's history up to the present. Most evocative is the re-created padre's bedroom with a thong-laced bed covered with a simple blanket, a writing table with quill pen in a glass ink stand, and a cracked leather chair.

After exploring the museum, pass through the gift shop and the courtyard and visit the church. It is a recent reconstruction of the 1809 chapel, which was destroyed in an earthquake in 1868. It houses some original artifacts that survived the quake, including a baptismal font of hammered copper.

Exiting through the other side of the church puts you in the mission's cemetery. The graves of Spanish, Mexican, and early Irish immigrants predominate.

Phone: (510) 657-1797.
Hours: Open daily 10 a.m. to 5 p.m.
Admission: $1.00 donation.
Parking: Free lot at the north end of the mission.
Wheelchair Access: Yes.

Mission Santa Clara

On the campus of Santa Clara University, Santa Clara.

The remains of this former Spanish mission are incorporated into the garden-like campus of Santa Clara University. The two go hand-in-hand, since the school opened in 1851 under the auspices of the local Franciscan priest, Joseph Alemany, who wanted to remedy the lack of educational institutions. Santa Clara University was the first institution of higher learning in California.

The mission was actually founded in 1777, a short distance away, but due to flooding and earthquakes was moved to the present site a few years later. The mission chapel dates from 1928. It's an enlarged version of the 1822 mission church, which was on the same site and was destroyed by fire in 1926.

A walk around the grounds will take you past some remnants of the earlier mission. Most notable are the Adobe Lodge and the attached adobe wall behind and to the side of the church. These two structures date from about 1822 and were the only survivors of the 1926 fire. The Adobe Lodge, which originally served as a priests' quarters, has been heavily remodeled, but the adobe wall with its coarse mud bricks evokes the earlier era.

Across from the mission is the **de Saisset Museum**. This attractive museum hosts changing exhibitions of paintings and sculpture by local and national artists. In the basement are some artifacts on permanent display from the 1822 mission. On view are a priest's vestments, silver containers for holy oil and baptismal water, and heavy iron church keys, to name a few.

Directions: From Highway 101, take the De La Cruz Boulevard/Santa Clara exit and follow the signs. The main campus entrance is at El Camino Real and Palm Drive. Information for the de Saisset Museum:
Phone: (408) 354-7159.
Hours: Tuesday - Sunday, 11 a.m. to 4 p.m.
Admission: Free.
Parking: Permits are available on Palm Drive as you enter the campus.
Wheelchair Access: Ground floor only.

Niles Railroad Depot and "Hollywood North"

36997 Mission Boulevard (three quarters of a mile north of Niles Canyon Road), Fremont.

Nestled in a sheltered valley at the south end of San Francisco Bay sits the historic Niles Depot. This railroad calendar pin-up, which dates from 1904, once served as an important junction for westbound transcontinental trains on their way to San Francisco.

The station was threatened with demolition in 1981 but was rescued by local rail enthusiasts. The building's interior houses various railroad memorabilia — a conductor's uniform, caps, matchbooks with train logos, and various mechanical devices.

The station also has an association with moviemaking history. California's first movie studio — the Essanay Studios — was built in the town of Niles, just the other side of the railroad tracks. It was here that "Bronco Billy" Anderson and a troupe of actors including a young Charlie Chaplin cranked out over 100 silent movies.

Many of the westerns used the Niles Depot as a backdrop. And it was in Niles that Chaplin first created his signature "Little Tramp" for the screen. Photographs on the wall inside the depot show the Essanay studios and Chaplin in Niles circa 1912.

The Essanay Studios building is gone but markers on the sidewalk on Niles Boulevard at G Street show where it stood. Some of the bungalows that Chaplin and the other actors used still stand at the back of the block. They are now private homes.

Phone: (510) 797-4449.
Hours: First and Third Sundays, 10 a.m. to 4 p.m.
Admission: Free. Donations appreciated.
Parking: Free.
Wheelchair Access: No.

The Octagon House

2645 Gough Street (at Union), San Francisco.

The Octagon House, dating from 1861, is one of the few Victorian homes in San Francisco that is open to the public. Its unusual shape was the result of a fad prevalent at the time: it was believed that an eight-sided building was more healthful for its occupants than a normal four-walled home, since it allegedly admitted more air and light. About 700 Octagon houses were built throughout the U.S.; this is one of only two left in San Francisco.

The interior of the house is furnished with Early American antiques, in keeping with the mission of the owner, the Colonial Dames of America, which is to preserve furniture and decorative arts of the Colonial and Federal periods (i.e., from the 18th and early 19th centuries). On display, for example, are a Chippendale mahogany sofa, a Hepplewhite sideboard, and a birds-eye maple grandfather clock. The oldest piece is a William and Mary table made in 1702.

One of the more interesting items is a deck of post-revolutionary playing cards. Having defeated the King of England, the colonists could not even tolerate having kings and queens on playing cards, so they made new ones. Kings became senators, queens became Greek goddesses, and jacks and knights became Indian chiefs.

Upstairs, secure behind glass, are signatures on documents of various kinds by all but two of the signers of the Declaration of Independence. All the famous names are here — Thomas Jefferson, Benjamin Franklin, John Hancock — as well as a host of lesser known ones.

Phone: (415) 441-7512.
Hours: Open only the 2nd Sunday and the 2nd and 4th Thursdays of the month from Noon until 3 p.m.
Admission: Free, but a donation of $2.00 is appreciated.
Parking: Neighborhood street parking only.
Wheelchair Access: No.

Old Mint

Fifth and Mission Streets, San Francisco.

This 1874 Greek Revival building, now a National Historic Landmark, was one of the few structures in downtown San Francisco to survive the 1906 earthquake and fire. It served as the west coast's primary mint until 1937 when the new mint on Duboce Street opened.

The Old Mint is now a museum; many of its rooms and vaults house exhibits on its history and on coins and coinage.

On the main floor you can see a half-hour movie about San Francisco and the mint, look at the restored superintendent's office, which has most of its original furninshings, and stamp your own souvenir medal from a large brass slug. The hallway walls are decorated with photographs, most showing the mint as it looked during construction and after the 1906 disaster.

In the basement are the vaults. This is where most of the bullion and coins were stored. Here you will find examples of gold-mining equipment — including an ore-crushing stamp mill, a re-creation of a gold miner's shack, and an exhibit on coinage that features a pile of silver dollars. In the room with the latter, notice the strange markings on the walls. These were made by silver dollars pressing through the coin bags that once filled the room.

The Old Mint has lately been threatened with closure, so call ahead to check its status.

Phone: (415) 744-6830.
Hours: Monday - Friday, 10 a.m. to 4 p.m. Closed holidays.
Self-guiding tours; also guided tours every hour on the half hour.
Due to financial problems the Mint might have to close, so call ahead.
Admission: Free.
Parking: There is a parking garage on the opposite corner of
5th and Mission.
Wheelchair Access: Yes.

Old St. Mary's Church

660 California Street (at Grant Avenue), San Francisco.

Old St. Mary's was the first cathedral erected in San Francisco. It was built in 1854 of granite blocks shipped from China, and bricks and ironwork that came around the Horn from New England. At a time when The City was still a mostly wood and canvas encampment, this brick building was the most prominent edifice in San Francisco and, indeed, on the entire West Coast.

The Gothic Revival-style church served as the seat of the San Francisco Catholic archdiocese until 1891. Partly to escape what was a deteriorating neighborhood, the archdiocese moved to tonier Van Ness Avenue that year. In 1894 St. Mary's came under the wing of the Paulist order of the Catholic Church, and remains so today, ministering to a largely Chinese congregation.

In 1906, St. Mary's, like the rest of downtown San Francisco, was destroyed by fire. The church's iron bell and marble altars melted due to the fire's intense heat, but the brick walls held, allowing for reconstruction within the original frame. The church was remodeled in the 1920s and again after a 1966 fire. The present facade thus looks slightly different from the 1854 original.

Note the biblical inscription on the belfry: "Son Observe the Time and Fly from Evil." This suitably Victorian approbation was directed at the patrons of the city's many brothels and opium dens, some of which, prior to 1906, stood directly across the street from the church.

History buffs will be interested to learn that the Emperor Norton, San Francisco's favorite 19th-century eccentric, dropped dead directly across the street from St. Mary's in January 1880.

Phone: (415) 986-4388.
Hours: To see the interior call for a schedule of masses.
Parking: St. Mary's Square garage across the street is closest.
Wheelchair Access: Yes.

The Palace of Fine Arts

3601 Lyon Street (between Bay and Jefferson), San Francisco.

The Palace of Fine Arts is the only building remaining from the Panama Pacific International Exposition, which is widely considered to have been the most beautiful and sucessful of San Francisco's three world fairs. The fair was held in 1915 along a one-mile stretch of the city's northern waterfront, extending from Fort Mason to Crissy Field.

The designer of the Palace of Fine Arts was the noted local architect Bernard Maybeck. The structure was intended as a paean to art and artists. To dramatize artistic struggles Maybeck designed a Greco-Romanesque rotunda and semicircular building (known as "The Shed"). His intent was to evoke an overgrown Roman ruin, and in that he succeeded perhaps too well. Fifty years after it was constructed, the original Palace, which was meant to be temporary and thus was built of *staff*, a mixture of plaster and burlap-type fiber over a wood frame, was looking like a real ruin. In the mid-1960s it was replaced by a concrete copy.

The Palace of Fine Arts today makes for one of San Francisco's most delightful green spaces. The placid lagoon — originally a frog pond where neighborhood children caught frogs and sold them to fishermen for bait — is home to swans and other waterfowl. The grassy lawn is studded with willows and other graceful trees. Little wonder then that it has served as a backdrop for numerous movies, fashion layouts, and weddings.

The north wing of The Shed houses The Exploratorium science museum (see p. 139).

Admission: The main rotunda is outdoors and is open to the public free of charge.
Parking: Street parking is usually available on Baker Street, which borders the Palace on the east.
Wheelchair Access: Yes.

Paramount Theatre

2025 Broadway (between 20th and 21st streets), Oakland.

"They don't build 'em like that anymore" is a well-worn cliché, but it fits the Paramount Theatre in spades. The Paramount is one of the few grand movie palaces remaining from the golden age of Hollywood — a time when moviegoing was as much of an experience as seeing the movie itself.

This extraordinary theatre is a stunning example of Art Deco style, a design that employed zigzags and swirls to great decorative effect. It opened on December 16, 1931, during the pit of the Depression, and, with its sumptuous furnishings, served almost as a counterpoint to the grim events of the day.

Despite its huge size, with its 3,000 seats and 90-foot-high ceilings, the theatre's interior has a surprisingly cozy feel. That perhaps is due to the subdued lighting and to its walls, which are painted in copper and gold leaf. The walls are embossed with stylized figures depicting such scenes as "The Princess" and "The Warrior." The dramatic Art Deco ceiling, bathed in a yellow light, also adds to the effect. It is known as "silver fins," and is made of an interlocking web of 12-gauge galvanized steel.

The Paramount Theatre currently hosts more than 150 events a year, ranging from film screenings to live stage shows. Most Friday nights they present "Paramount Movie Classics," showings of past major motion pictures. To see *Citizen Kane* or *Wuthering Heights* in this theatre is the closest you'll ever come to going back in time 50 years.

Access: Tours start at the theatre box office on 21st Street between Broadway and Telegraph Avenue.
Phone: (510) 893-2300.
Hours: Docent-led tours given on the 1st and 3rd Saturdays of the month at 10 a.m. sharp.
Admission: $1.00 per person.
Parking: There are lots next to the theatre and on Telegraph at 21st Street.
Wheelchair Access: Main floor only.

Pardee Home

672 11th Street (at Castro), Oakland.

This Italianate villa, located not far from downtown Oakland, was the home of George C. Pardee, governor of California at the time of the 1906 earthquake and fire. It was lived in by three generations of Pardees, from its construction in 1868 until 1981.

The house has been left just the way it was when the last Pardee died in 1981; thus the interior furnishings reflect a mix of styles ranging from Victorian to that of the 1950s, when a last remodeling was done. This has led to some odd juxtapositions: a Victorian desk frames one side of a door and a 1939 big-box radio the other; a gramaphone points its horn at a color TV.

The governor's wife was a collector of various knicknacks — candlesticks, teacups, and Chinese figurines to name a few, and these cover tabletops and mantlepieces throughout, giving the house a magpie decor. Much of it is 19th-century kitsch, but many museums would readily kill for some things, such as the large collection of Alaskan scrimshaw.

A most unusual object and truly a one-of-a-kind item is a lamp suspended from the ceiling in the main hallway. It is a six-sided box illuminated from within and made up of two-foot-square photos etched on glass. The photos are original views of Yosemite by the 19th-century photographer Carleton Watkins.

Upstairs you can view the bedrooms and learn more about the family. The docent will likely show you a copy of a chap book kept by one of the teenage daughters, in which she rated and commented on her suitors. One such would-be paramour was dismissed as "too dirty, teeth are green."

Phone: (510) 444-2187.
Hours: Guided tours given Thursday, Friday, and Saturday at 11 a.m., 1 p.m., and 2:30 p.m. Reservations are required.
Admission: Adults $4.00; Seniors $3.00; Children under 12, Free.
Parking: Free and metered street parking available nearby.
Wheelchair Access: No.

Patterson House and Ardenwood Historic Farm

34600 Ardenwood Blvd. (off Highway 84), Fremont.

Of all the landmark historic houses mentioned in this book, the George W. Patterson House is arguably the best preserved and most "authentic." This is helped by the fact that this 1889 Queen Anne Victorian is still furnished with the Patterson family's belongings. Walking through the rooms you almost feel as if you're an interloper — that the Pattersons will return any moment.

What makes this property even more interesting are the surrounding grounds, which have been re-created as a turn-of-the-century working farm. Volunteer docents dressed in Victorian clothing work at the estate. Some give tours of the house, others demonstrate farm chores.

Most weekends you can get a tour of the whole farm in wagons drawn by sturdy Belgian draft horses. Some periodic special events include such things as animal feedings, horseshoeing demonstrations, and "Wash Day on the Farm," where you can learn how laundry was done in the 19th century.

There is a farmyard cafe where period food and drinks are served, but you are free to bring your own picnic lunches. In keeping with the historic nature of the park, no barbecues are allowed, and modern playthings such as frisbees, footballs, and soccer balls are not permitted. Dogs are also prohibited.

If you have time while you are in the area, only a short distance away is Coyote Hills Regional Park (see p. 89).

Phone: (510) 796-0663.
Hours: Open April through mid-November, Thursday - Sunday, 10 a.m. to 5 p.m. (gate closes at 4 p.m.) Also open in December for Christmas tours. Note: Rain may close the farm without notice.
Admission: Adults $5.00; Seniors (62+) $3.00; Children (4–17) $2.50.
Parking: Free.
Wheelchair Access: Yes for the grounds, no for the house.

Petaluma Adobe

3325 Adobe Road (at Casa Grande), Petaluma.

The Petaluma Adobe is the largest and most restored of the few remaining Mexican-era adobes in northern California. It served as the headquarters for former San Francisco Presidio commandante General Mariano Vallejo on what was once a 66,000-acre ranch.

The Adobe was constructed during a 10-year period starting in 1836. It was nearly complete when it was raided in 1846 by U.S. Army Captain John C. Fremont during the infamous Bear Flag Revolt, a short-lived attempt to wrest California from Mexico and turn it into an independent republic.

Fremont stripped the ranch of its horses, cattle, and various provisions, which led to a progressive decline that stopped only in the 1950s when a restoration effort was begun. By that time all of the original furnishings were gone and the eastern half of the building had disintegrated.

Today the surviving western half of the structure has been restored and refurbished with replicas and period pieces. The few remaining acres bordering the ranch have been converted to a working farm.

Highlights of the interior include the ranch foreman's room with its bed, writing table, and a saddle resting on its stand, and the tallow and hide workroom with its candle dipping machine. Also not to be missed are the Vallejo family apartments. The dining room in particular gives a vivid picture of the graciousness of the life led by the landed gentry.

Directions: From Highway 101 in Sonoma County take Highway 116 east for four miles.
Phone: (707) 762-4871.
Hours: Open daily 10 a.m. to 5 p.m.
Admission: Adults $2.00; Children (6–17) $1.00; under 6, Free.
Parking: Free.
Wheelchair Access: Yes, except for the second floor.

Ralston Hall

1500 Ralston Avenue (between El Camino Real and Alameda de las Pulgas), Belmont.

William Ralston was, in the 1860s and '70s, owner of some of the richest silver mines in Nevada. Befitting his wealth, he built what eventually grew to be a 55,000-square-foot house on a 100-acre country estate south of San Francisco. Ralston's Nob Hill mansion and his famous Palace Hotel burned in 1906 but this, his country estate in Belmont, still survives.

After Ralston died prematurely, in 1875, his partner, William Sharon, claimed title and carried on Ralston's tradition of lavish entertaining. At one such gathering, a tribute to former president Ulysses S. Grant in 1879, 1,800 guests consumed 15,000 oysters and 100 cases of champagne.

The house's interior has changed little since the days of Ralston and Sharon. A highlight is the music room with its large framed mirrors and wood parquet floors. Upstairs is a beautiful loge, modeled after a larger one in the Paris Opera. Notice the silver plated rails and fittings, emblematic of Ralston's silver fortune. The loge also contains some Ralston family photos and a few of their original furnishings.

After the Ralston/Sharon era the estate was eventually purchased by the Sisters of Notre Dame de Namur, who use the building as the nucleus of their College of Notre Dame campus. They open Ralston Hall periodically for various functions and public tours.

Phone: (415) 593-1601, ext. 501.
Hours: Docent-led tours are given irregularly, usually only on weekdays. Call Monday - Friday, 9 a.m. to 4 p.m., for information and reservations.
Admission: Adults $5.00; Seniors and Students $3.00.
Parking: Inquire when you call for reservations.
Wheelchair Access: Yes.

Robert Dollar Mansion and Falkirk Cultural Center

1408 Mission Avenue (at E Street), San Rafael.

This large Queen Anne Victorian house, constructed in 1888, provides a glimpse of what country estate living must have been like in the late 19th century. Situated on 11 acres, it has been listed on the National Register of Historic Places since 1972.

Since none of the original furniture remains, the house is furnished with period pieces and antiques. The wood-paneled walls, however, are still faced with their original Sierra pine, burled ash, and redwood. A picture window on the second floor affords a view of downtown San Rafael.

The house was first owned by Ella Park, a wealthy widow. In 1906, after her death the previous year, the property was purchased by Robert Dollar, who started life as a penniless Scotsman but built a fortune in lumber and shipping. Dollar named his estate Falkirk, after his hometown in Scotland.

Falkirk today serves as a cultural center for the local community. The second floor of the mansion has been converted to an art gallery, which houses changing art and photography exhibitions. The grounds, studded with oak, magnolia, and exotic bunya-bunya trees, serve as a public park.

Phone: (415) 485-3328.
Hours: Tuesday, Wednesday, and Friday, 10 a.m. to 4:30 p.m.;
Thursday, 10 a.m. to 9 p.m.; Saturday, 10 a.m. to 1 p.m.
Admission: Free, but suggested donation: Adults $2.00; Seniors $1.00.
Parking: Free lot at the end of E Street.
Wheelchair Access: Yes.

Sanchez Adobe

1000 Linda Mar Boulevard (at Adobe Road), Pacifica.

Tucked away in a fertile valley not far from the ocean sits a seldom-visited historic landmark — the Sanchez Adobe. This restored two-story adobe and wood building was constructed between 1842 and 1846 for Don Francisco Sanchez, a Mexican land grantee and three-time alcalde (mayor) of San Francisco.

The history of the site goes back much farther. It was the location, probably for centuries, of an Ohlone Indian village. This came in handy for the Spanish, who in 1786 established a farm here to supply foodstuffs to Mission Dolores in San Francisco; the Native Americans were pressed into service as laborers. But by 1792 the farm's viability was at an end, since most of the Indians had succumbed to disease.

After Francisco Sanchez died in 1862 the adobe and its acreage were sold to a Civil War general. After his tenure, the building served variously as a hotel, hunting lodge, quarters for artichoke farm field workers, and finally as a speakeasy. In short, the property encompasses much of the history of California.

Inside the adobe, which was restored in 1953 to its 1840s appearance, are various period artifacts used to replicate a main parlor, bedrooms, and others. The only original relics, which were uncovered during recent archeological excations, are on view in two glass display cases on the main floor. Here you can see stone tools used by the Indians, ceramic pottery fragments, and even an intact ginger-beer bottle circa 1860.

Phone: (415) 359-1462.
Hours: Saturday and Sunday, 1 p.m. to 5 p.m.; Tuesday - Thursday, 10 a.m. to 4 p.m.
Admission: Free.
Parking: Free lot on the premises.
Restrooms: Yes.
Wheelchair Access: Ground floor only.

Shinn House

1251 Peralta Avenue (at Sidney), Fremont.

The Shinn House is a prime example of a Victorian farmhouse. It was lived in by three generations of Shinns and their spouses from 1876 to 1968. The first generation established a successful farm and pioneer nursery.

The interior of of the house, which had succumbed to vandalism after the death of the last occupant, has been restored to show what it looked like in the 1880s. About one third of the furnishings are the Shinns', the rest are period pieces that were donated or are on loan. As a rarity among historic houses, you are actually allowed to touch the clothing and sit on the furniture.

In contrast to Victorian-era excess found in grander houses of the time, the Shinn House reflects the tastes of a hard-working farm family. No expensive woods were used and the fireplaces are not elaborate.

But with a flair for the unusual, the Shinns used Japanese screens as wallpaper in the boys' bedroom upstairs. The floors in this bedroom and the others are covered by tatami mats. Newspapers were placed under these, docents explain, because the lead in the ink helped control fleas.

Only a few acres remain of what was originally a 300-acre ranch, but you can stroll the grounds and admire the rare and exotic trees, including a huge Moreton Bay fig tree just to the west of the house. The Japanese garden — a 20th-century addition — provides pathways for a soothing stroll among bonsai and other shrubbery.

Phone: (510) 656-9076.
Hours: Open only the first Wednesday and the third Sunday of the month from 1 to 3 p.m.
Admission: Adults $3.00; Children and Seniors $1.50.
Parking: Free lot in front of the house.
Wheelchair Access: Yes for the grounds and the ground floor of the house.

Tao House - Eugene O'Neill National Historic Site

In the hills behind Danville, Contra Costa County.

Tao House was once the home of Eugene O'Neill, the only American playwright to win the Nobel Prize (he also won four Pulitzer prizes). O'Neill and his wife Carlotta lived here from 1937 to 1944, and it was here that O'Neill wrote some of his greatest plays, including *Long Day's Journey Into Night* and *A Moon for the Misbegotten*.

O'Neill came to the West Coast seeking seclusion so that he could write. He chose a spot high in the hills above Danville and, in 1937, built this concrete house with a Spanish tile roof. He called it Tao House because he had an interest in Taoism, an ancient Chinese philosophy.

The property is now owned by the National Park Service. Park rangers give guided tours of the house. All of the main rooms are part of the tour, but the dwelling is mostly bare since only a few furnishings and personal possessions of O'Neill's remain.

The home's interior has a sterile feel to it, perhaps because of its emptiness, but the playwright's study, where he did his writing, is the exception. A cozy enclave with a fireplace, a sunporch, and a view of Mt. Diablo, it is furnished with two desks similar to the ones he had, his own chair, and some of his personal effects. A curiosity is a sample of O'Neill's handwriting — so minuscule as to be indecipherable.

Directions: You are driven to the site from a Danville parking lot in a Park Service van. Call the following number for reservations and directions.
Phone: (510) 838-0249.
Hours: Tours are given Wednesday - Sunday at 10 a.m. and 12:30 p.m.
Admission: Free.
Parking: Free.
Wheelchair Access: Yes, except for the house's second floor (where the living quarters and O'Neill's study are).

Villa Montalvo

15400 Montalvo Road, Saratoga.

Nestled in the foothills of the Santa Cruz mountains is Villa Montalvo, the country estate of former San Francisco mayor and U.S. Senator James D. Phelan. Phelan hosted visiting writers, artists, and celebrities here from 1912 until his death in 1930. He left the property in trust to the people of California with the wish that it be used to further the arts.

The property today has two theaters, including an outdoor amphitheater, an art gallery, and an artists-in-residence program. During the summer, Villa Montalvo is the setting for a series of popular outdoor concerts. Performers who have appeared here include Dave Brubeck, Los Lobos, and the Preservation Hall Jazz Band.

Separate from the creative and performing arts aspect are the grounds of this 175-acre estate. They are open to the public most days. Fronting the mansion is a manicured sloping green lawn surrounded by magnolias, maples, cedars, oaks, and other trees and shrubbery. There are also three miles of hiking trails leading through the woods in the hills behind the house.

Guided tours of Phelan's Mediterranean-style villa are given twice a week from April to September. You will see the interior of this beautiful home and learn more about the life and lifestyle of this witty and cultured man.

Directions: From Highway 9 in Saratoga turn on Montalvo Road and follow the signs.
Phone: (408) 741-3421.
Hours: The grounds are open Monday - Friday, 8 a.m. to 5 p.m.; Saturday and Sunday, 9 a.m. to 5 p.m. Tours of the villa are given Thursdays and Saturdays at 10 a.m. from April through September.
Admission: The grounds are free; house tours are: Adults $5.00; Seniors and Children $3.00.
Parking: Free.
Wheelchair Access: Yes for the art gallery and some of the grounds, no for the villa.

Woodside Store

Located at the intersection of Kings Mountain Road and Tripp Road near Woodside, 35 miles south of San Francisco.

The Woodside Store is a rare commercial building surviving from the gold-rush era. It is probably the only one in the Bay Area made of wood, and likely owes its longevity to its relatively remote location in a wooded canyon in a semi-rural area.

It was constructed in 1854, and until 1909 served as a combination general store, post office, stagecoach stop, and livery stable. In its heyday it was a crossroads location, serving as a transit stop between the lumber mills that dotted the area and the port of Redwood City, where sawed lumber was hauled by teams of oxen.

The building is made of rough-sawed, unpainted redwood, and stands as an eloquent monument to the plain, hard-working men and women who carved new lives out of the wilderness.

The interior has a solid, well-worn wooden counter top in front of shelves stocked with all manner of goods — baking powder, bottles of wine, coffee pots, Bull Durham tobacco, bolts of cloth, and hats, to name a few. Many of the artifacts are replicas, but in the back room are some original pieces, including wooden mallets, a leather strop, plow harnesses, and an ox yoke.

A small room at the side of the building has some other Victorian artifacts, most notably an 1850 dentist chair. It likely belonged to Dr. Robert O. Tripp, the country storekeeper who was also the community's dentist.

Directions: From Highway 280 take the Woodside Road (Highway 84) exit heading west. Follow Woodside Road to Kings Mountain Road, turn right and go .7 mile.
Phone: (415) 851-7615.
Hours: Tuesday and Thursday, 10 a.m. to 4 p.m.; Saturday and Sunday, 12 Noon to 4 p.m.
Admission: Free.
Parking: Free lot.
Wheelchair Access: Yes.

Parks

The Golden Gate Bridge as seen from San Francisco's
newest park—the Presidio.

Alamo Square

**Bounded by Fulton, Steiner, Hayes, and Scott streets
in San Francisco's Western Addition.**

Located in a neighborhood not known for tourist attractions, Alamo Square offers one of the most reproduced views of San Francisco — that of "postcard row." This image of Victorian row houses in the foreground with the downtown skyline in the background has been reproduced on countless postcards, calendars, and posters. The view is from the southeast corner of Alamo Square.

Fortunately for those who like views, most of San Francisco's parks in the western part of the city are located on high ground. This is a legacy of city planning in the nineteenth century, when hilltops were not considered valuable land since they were difficult to build on with the available technology. Thus west of Van Ness Avenue many of the promontories were reserved as public land, later to be designated as parks.

Alamo Square was nothing more than a windswept sandy hill until 1892, when the city graded and landscaped it, turning it into a real park for the first time. After the 1906 earthquake and fire Alamo Square served briefly as a campground for the homeless.

Today the park is one of sloping green lawns dotted with mature pine, eucalyptus, and willow trees. Broad paved paths wind throughout; green-painted wooden benches are placed at regular intervals. Development has walled off most of the views of the bay that could once be had from its summit, but the park still affords views west toward Buena Vista Park and the University of California at San Francisco, north toward Alta Plaza, and, looking northeast, the view of "postcard row."

Amenities include a tennis court, a picnic table, and a childrens' playground; all are located near the center of the park.

Restrooms: No.
Wheelchair Access: Yes. The easiest is from the corner of Fulton and Scott.

Alta Plaza

Bounded by Jackson, Steiner, Clay, and Scott streets in San Francisco's
Pacific Heights neighborhood.

Alta Plaza is a four-block-square park located in Pacific
Heights amidst some of the city's choicest residential real estate.
Because it spans the southern ridge of Pacific Heights's crest, on
its Clay and Steiner street sides it is a ziggurat of stepped embank-
ments punctuated by paved walkways at each rise. Its Jackson
Street side more or less is at ground level.

The park boundaries were delineated in 1855 when it became
part of the Western Addition, a huge extension of the city past its
original Larkin Street border. Alta Plaza is one of seven such large
squares, and is one of the two major parks in Pacific Heights (the
other is Lafayette Park).

The park has a number of attractions, not the least of which are
the views to be had from its summit. The best views are those
looking south. Here is a sweep of central San Francisco from the
Civic Center on the left to the spires of St. Ignatius Church at the
University of San Francisco on the right. To the north, most of the
scene is blocked by the large homes on Jackson Street, but from a
bench facing Pierce Street there is a view down over the Marina
and the bay, and to Tiburon in the distance.

Alta Plaza has three tennis courts, a basketball half-court, and
a tree-shaded children's playground surrounded by a low fence.
The well-used playground has a full complement of swings,
slides, and wooden platforms for climbing. The playground, and
the whole park, has plenty of benches for sitting and sunning. The
broad, relatively flat lawn in the northwest corner of the park is a
popular sunbathing spot on warm days.

Restrooms: Yes (near the childrens' playground), but the doors are
usually locked.
Wheelchair Access: Limited. Best points of entry would be at the
corners of Jackson and Scott or Jackson and Steiner, but there are
no cutouts to facilitate access.

Angel Island State Park

Located in San Francisco Bay off the Tiburon peninsula.

Angel Island is notable for two reasons: it is rich in history, and it offers unique views of the bay and the surrounding cities.

Public ferry service drops you at Ayala Cove, named for the Spanish explorer who anchored here in 1775 while mapping the bay. The cove area has a visitor center, picnic area, and a snack bar.

You might start your exploration of the island by hiking to the summit, **Mt. Livermore.** There is a 360-degree panoramic view from here: the magnificent bay surrounds on all sides, lapping at the shores of San Francisco, Oakland and Berkeley in the distance, and Tiburon and Sausalito closer by.

Down by the shoreline, the Perimeter Trail circles the island and winds past the main areas of historical interest, mainly military fortifications. Moving in a counter clockwise direction from Ayala Cove you will first come to **Camp Reynolds,** noteworthy for its fine collection of wooden Civil War-era buildings.

On the opposite side of the island is **East Garrison,** also known as **Fort McDowell.** A military garrison from 1898 until 1946, during World War II Fort McDowell had the distinction of being the biggest induction center in the United States. The largely Mission Revival-style buildings now stand empty, awaiting restoration.

North Garrison, or **Immigration Station,** served from 1910 to 1940 as the "Ellis Island of the West." It mainly served as an entry point for Chinese immigrants. The barracks now serve as a museum documenting the loneliness and despair they felt as they awaited clearance to enter the country.

Phones: Ayala Cove (415) 435-3522; Red & White Fleet, from San Francisco, (800) 229-2784; McDonough Ferry, from Tiburon, (415) 435-2131.
Hours and Admission: Call for ferry departure and return times and tolls. Fees range from $8.00 for adults to $3.00 for children.
Restrooms: Yes.
Wheelchair Access: Yes for the cove area and the Perimeter Trail.

Anthony Chabot Regional Park

The park occupies the ridgetop in the East Bay hills above San Leandro.

This nearly 5,000-acre park offers a network of trails open to hikers, joggers, runners, equestrians, and bicyclists. A prime attraction other than the chance to commune with nature is Lake Chabot and its marina.

The park and the lake are named for Anthony Chabot, a pioneer businessman and engineer who created this lake in 1874 and 1875 by building a dam. The lake serves today as a reserve water supply for the city of Oakland.

At the marina you can rent canoes, pedal boats, rowboats, and electric boats for use on the lake. Swimming is not allowed but fishing is. Fishing licenses are required. If you don't have one you can buy a daily permit for $2.50 at the snack bar.

In the vicinity of the marina is a family recreation area. There is a volleyball net, two horseshoe pits, and lots of picnic tables and barbecue grills.

For those who can't get their fill of hiking at Anthony Chabot, Redwood Regional Park, which adjoins Chabot to the north, has several more miles of trails. In the 19th century it was the site of major logging operations. Today the sawmills are gone but the stately redwoods remain.

Directions: From Interstate 580 take the Fairmount Drive exit east toward the hills. Fairmount becomes Lake Chabot Road; continue south a short distance and turn left into the Lake Chabot entrance.
Phone: The marina's number is (510) 582-2198.
Hours: The marina is open from 7 a.m. to 6 p.m; other parts of the park, including the campgrounds east of the lake, are open later.
Admission and **Parking:** The park itself is free but the parking lot at the marina costs $3.00 when the kiosk is attended, $2.00 other times (bring quarters). If you don't want to pay for parking you can park for free on Lake Chabot Road outside the entrance.
Restrooms: Yes.
Wheelchair Access: Partial. Trails near the lake are wheelchair accessible.

Black Diamond Mines Regional Preserve

Located 35 miles east of San Francisco and just south of Antioch in Contra Costa County.

A coal mine near San Francisco Bay? It's true.

This little-known park was, in the 19th century, the site of a large coal-mining operation. From the 1850s until 1902 over 100 miles of tunnels produced nearly four million tons of coal ("black diamonds"). Believe it or not, sand (it was used for making glass) was also mined here.

Today you can hike trails leading throughout this 3,700 acre preserve and see mine entrances, air shafts, and a powder magazine. A couple of the mine entrances are even open for the first 50 or 100 feet. Bring a flashlight.

This is hilly country; some of the trails are rather steep, so hiking boots or athletic shoes are a must. If you hike up beyond the Somersville townsite area at the end of the paved road you will be surprised at how the scenery changes from rolling grassy hills to rocky outcroppings surrounded by manzanita and chaparral. Certain vistas look more like Wyoming than the East Bay.

Don't miss seeing the Rose Hill cemetery. It serves as a poignant reminder of how hard life was in the not too distant past. Here you will find grave markers of men killed in mine accidents, but the graves of children predominate. Many succumbed to periodic epidemics of diptheria, typhoid, or scarlet fever.

Directions: From Highway 4, take the Somersville Road exit south two miles and continue straight where the road curves to the left.
Phone: (510) 757-2620.
Hours: Open daily 8 a.m. to 5 p.m.
Admission: Free.
Parking: Free.
Restrooms: Yes.
Wheelchair Access: No.

Buena Vista Park

The park is located several blocks south of the Golden Gate Park Panhandle and is bounded by Haight Street, Yerba Buena West, and Yerba Buena East.

Buena Vista or "Good View" got its name from Spanish settlers who first climbed to its summit in the 18th century. Sparsely covered with vegetation at that time, it commanded a sweeping 360-degree view.

A favorite viewpoint for 19th-century visitors, it was reserved as a park in 1868. About 1910, John McLaren, superintendent of Golden Gate Park, started planting many of the trees — eucalyptus, Monterey Cypress, and Monterey Pine — that have now turned this into a miniature forest.

Today, by looking past the trees and neighboring buildings, you can still see some of the distant views that enchanted earlier San Franciscans. To gain an initial overview and see some of the best vistas, take the wide paved path to the summit; it starts near the intersection of Buena Vista West and Upper Terrace Street. Once there, you'll be surprised to find how high you are relative to the rest of the city. There are especially good views of the Western Addition, Pacific Heights, and the Golden Gate Bridge.

There are other vista points, most notably at "The Overlook," but the other main feature here is that, if you don't mind some steep grades, this is a good park for hiking. There are several paved paths, and for the more athletic there are some narrow dirt trails that wind all over. In the northern, lower part of the park the main paved path takes you through a stand of redwood trees; adjacent to it is a grove of native coast live oaks.

The park also has a couple of tennis courts, a children's playground, green wooden benches, and a couple of picnic tables.

Restrooms: No.
Wheelchair Access: Partial. Entry limited to the intersection of Buena Vista West and Upper Terrace Street and the short paved path to the summit.

Candlestick Park

Along the shoreline behind the stadium, in southeast San Francisco.

Bay Area residents know Candlestick Park as the home of the major league San Francisco Giants baseball team and the pro football Forty-Niners. Few realize that bordering the stadium is a state park.

Officially known as Candlestick Point State Recreation Area, it hugs the shoreline east and south of the stadium and consists of land reclaimed from San Francisco Bay. Although the park is within sight of the 101 freeway, it is far enough away that you can't hear the traffic noise, making it more quiet and peaceful than might be expected.

A network of trails, both dirt and paved and suitable for hiking, jogging, and bicycling, lead out to a little peninsula at the east end of the park. The shore of the cove between the peninsula's knob and the main shore is a good spot for birdwatching. Brown pelicans, grebes, and egrets are some of the birds seen here.

The park has a good number of picnic tables and there are two fishing piers along the southern shoreline. Fishing from the piers does not require a license.

It is said that Candlestick Point got its name from pioneer ship salvors who used this area to burn gold-rush ships in order to retrieve brass fittings and other metals from the vessels. The flaming masts sinking into the water looked like candlesticks.

Directions: From Highway 101 take the Candlestick Park exit and follow the road toward the stadium parking lots. Look for the park's entrance off to the right.
Phone: (415) 557-2593.
Hours: Open daily 8 a.m. to sunset.
Admission: Free except on game days at the stadium; fees then are $8.00 for Giants games and $12.00 for Niners games.
Parking: Free.
Restrooms: Yes.
Wheelchair Access: Yes.

China Camp State Park

On the Marin shoreline northeast of San Rafael.

The main attraction here is the historic and almost deserted Chinese fishing village. In the 19th century, when San Francisco Bay teemed with shrimp, Chinese fishermen harvested huge quantities of them from nets cast from their junks and from shore. China Camp is not only the last survivor of what were once more than 30 such camps in the Bay Area, but it is believed to be the last one in California.

China Camp's heyday was the 1870s when this shoreline fishing village numbered 500 people. By the 1880s it began to decline. Today, Frank Quan, a descendant of the camp's early pioneers, carries on, netting shrimp from his small boat.

A few rustic wooden buildings remain huddled at the water's edge. The weathered board shed jutting out over the water houses a small museum. The artifacts and the accompanying photographs and descriptive panels chart the camp's history and the statutory discrimination that led to its decline. Most evocative is a re-creation of a storage area piled with baskets of shrimp, nets, and coils of rope.

You don't have to be a history buff to appreciate China Camp, however. Set where it is, in a secluded cove, it's a beautiful spot for a picnic, particularly in the late afternoon when the sun will be behind you as you gaze out over the bay. There are picnic tables on the bluff at the village's entrance.

Directions: From Highway 101 in San Rafael, exit at either North San Pedro Road or at Third Street, which becomes Point San Pedro Road, and follow the signs for about eight miles to the entrance to the fishing village.
Phone: (415) 456-0766 or 456-1286.
Hours: The park is open daily 8 a.m. to sunset, and the museum is open 10 a.m. to 5 p.m.
Admission: Free.
Parking: There is a free gravel lot in front of the village.
Restrooms: Yes.
Wheelchair Access: Yes.

Coyote Hills Regional Park

8000 Patterson Ranch Road (off Paseo Padre Parkway), Fremont.

This pleasant park, located not far from the shore of San Francisco Bay, offers a chance to visit an Indian shellmound and to explore a marshland bird sanctuary via a network of trails.

The place to start is the visitor center, which is located about a mile up the road from the park entrance. Here you will find a number of attractive displays on the Native Americans — the Ohlone — who inhabited this site for over two thousand years. There are also lifelike re-created habitats of the various birds, waterfowl, and deer that live in the park.

The shellmound, near which sits a reconstructed Ohlone village, is well worth a visit. Park rangers give guided tours that explain the lifeways of the Ohlone and how the shellmound, which is composed of discarded shells and animal bones, has also yielded evidence of at least five hundred human burials. Tours of the shellmound are only given on selected weekends. Reservations are a must.

Most of the hiking trails leave from the vicinity of the visitor center. Across the road from the center is the main marsh, which has several flat, broad trails leading through it. Behind the visitor center are trails that take you up along the ridge. From here there are good views of the marsh on one side and San Francisco Bay on the other.

The grassy lawn in front of the visitor center is a popular picnic spot; there are picnic tables and barbecue pits.

Phone: (510) 795-9385.
Hours: The park itself is open daily 8 a.m. to sunset; the visitor center, Tuesday - Sunday, 9:30 a.m. to 5 p.m. Shellmound tours are given Saturdays or Sundays once or twice a month. Call in advance to make reservations.
Admission and **Parking:** $3.00 per vehicle.
Wheelchair Access: Yes for the visitor center and the lowland trails.

Fort Mason

On the northern shoreline of San Francisco. The main entrance is via
Franklin Street.

Fort Mason is the headquarters for the Golden Gate National
Recreation Area (Building #201). Although the eastern portion of
the fort is still an active military post, the grounds are open to the
public. The northwest corner, Fort Mason Center, is home to over
50 non-profit cultural and educational organizations.

Of interest among the military's remaining buildings — which
consist mainly of housing — are the officers quarters: some of
them date back to 1855, placing them among the oldest houses in
San Francisco. The three oldest (all dating from the 1850s) are the
residences numbered 2, 3, and 4 on the east side of Franklin Street.
All three have superb views of the bay.

Walk west on Funston Street from the end of Franklin and you
will come to a former Civil War-era barracks that is now a youth
hostel. Behind it are scooped-out earthworks that once held a gun
battery.

You can reach Fort Mason Center from the hostel by following
the paved road to the left and descending a long flight of stairs to
the parking lot. There is also an automobile entrance across from
the Safeway on Buchanan Street.

Fort Mason Center is home to a variety of museums (see p. 12),
craft organizations, and music, theater, and dance companies.
They occupy former warehouses and piers that during World War
II served as a staging area for troops shipping out for Pacific
battlefields. The *Jeremiah O'Brien* (see p. 126), one of two surviving
World War II Liberty ships — riding at anchor next to Pier 3 —
serves as a reminder of this wartime heritage.

Phone: (415) 556-0560 (GGNRA headquarters).
Hours: Open daily 8 a.m. to sunset. Organizations at
Fort Mason Center have their own hours.
Parking: Free lots at both locations.
Wheelchair Access: Yes.

Golden Gate National Recreation Area

The park covers much of western Marin County and most of the northern and western shoreline of San Francisco.

The Golden Gate National Recreation Area (GGNRA) is the largest urban park in the world. Encompassing terrain ranging from mountain peaks to valleys, bays, and the ocean, it offers breathtaking scenery — most of it left in its natural state.

The park hugs much of the coastline outside the Golden Gate and extends from Point Reyes National Seashore 20+ miles north of San Francisco to Sweeney Ridge 15 miles south. Major portions are accessible by car, but hikers will enjoy the hundreds of miles of trails. There are historic forts, gun batteries, and lighthouses to explore, and you'll be able to enjoy up close the diverse vegetation and some of the wildlife, including deer, heron, and hawks.

Some of the attractions mentioned elsewhere in this book — such as Alcatraz, Fort Point, and Mt. Tamalpais, to name a few — fall within the GGNRA's boundaries. Also worthy of note is the drive along Conzelman Road in the Marin Headlands just north and west of the Golden Gate Bridge. All along this five-mile stretch are breathtaking views of the Golden Gate Bridge, the entrance to the bay, and San Francisco.

This only scratches the surface of the riches to be found in this park. Pick up a copy of the GGNRA's *Park Guide*. It's available at the GGNRA headquarters at Fort Mason (Building 201), at some of the park's other locations, and at most bookstores.

Phone: (415) 556-0560 (GGNRA HQ).
Hours: Park lands are open daily 8 a.m. to sunset. Individual attractions within the park have separate hours.
Admission: Most of the park is free, but places such as Muir Woods and Alcatraz charge admission fees.
Parking: Free at all the visitor centers and most parts of the park.
Restrooms: All visitor centers have restrooms.
Wheelchair Access: Check with individual locations.

Golden Gate Park — Eastern Half

The whole of Golden Gate Park is bordered by Lincoln Way, the Great
Highway, and Fulton and Stanyan streets in San Francisco. The eastern
half extends from Stanyan Street to Cross-Over Drive.

Golden Gate Park is one of San Francisco's great resources. You
can go to visit its museums, to play baseball, golf, or tennis, to ride
bikes, roller skate, or horseback ride, to picnic, to sunbathe, or just
to walk its many paths, paved and unpaved, to enjoy its wealth of
greenery and scenery.

It occupies a three-mile-long and half-mile-wide rectangle in
the western half of the city. Until 1870 this land was nothing but
desolate sand dunes. Landscaping began in the eastern end of the
park that year and slowly moved westward, continuing for decades. Today, Golden Gate Park ranks as the world's largest landscaped park — bigger even than New York's Central Park.

The eastern end of the park attracts the most visitors because
it has three museums and the park's other major landmarks and
attractions. They are all written up separately elsewhere in this
book: **Asian Art Museum** (p. 3); **California Academy of Sciences**
(p. 6); **M.H. de Young Memorial Museum** (p. 11); **Conservatory
of Flowers** (p. 50); **Japanese Tea Garden** (p. 97); **Strybing Arboreteum** (p. 111); and the **Children's Playground** (p. 137).

There are plenty of other things worthy of your attention in the
park's eastern half. Here's a brief rundown:

Stow Lake, which is the largest lake in the park, forms a ring
around an island known as Strawberry Hill. Two bridges lead
over to the island and a broad trail winds to the summit. Once
there, you will be surprised at how high up you are. There are
great views of the city through the trees in all directions except to
the west. Down below, Stow Lake's boathouse rents rowboats,
pedal boats, and electric motor boats by the hour.

Just across JFK Drive north of the boathouse is **Prayerbrook
Cross** and **Rainbow Falls**. This 57-foot-high Celtic cross, at the
top of the falls, was built in 1894 as part of the Midwinter Fair of

that year, which was held in Golden Gate Park. It commemorates the first religious service held on these shores — by Sir Francis Drake's chaplain during Drake's stopover on the California coast in 1579. Rainbow Falls was constructed in the 1930s.

If you walk east from the falls along JFK Drive, on the left side you'll soon come to the **Redwood Memorial Grove**. Both here and just on the other side of the Rose Garden a trail winds through a grove of redwood trees. Despite the fact that this little forest is close to the highway you'll be surprised at how quiet and peaceful it is.

The **Rose Garden** has over a dozen formal beds planted with roses of every conceivable color, bearing such names as Scarlet Knight, Iceberg, Gold Medal, Brigadoon, and Roman Holiday.

Go farther along JFK Drive, and once past 8th Avenue, on the right side, you'll come to the **John McLaren Rhododendron Dell**. McLaren was the park's superintendent from 1887 until his death at age 96 in 1943. This was McLaren's favorite part of Golden Gate Park. A network of trails covering over 200 acres will take you past literally hundreds of hybrid species of rhododendrons as well as other plants and trees.

Just east and south of the tennis courts, which are across Middle Drive East at the eastern end of the dell, is **Sharon Meadow**. The mounded portion to the north was known as "Hippie Hill" during the 1960s, because it was a favorite gathering spot for flower children from nearby Haight-Ashbury.

To accurately find your way around the park, pick up a copy of the *Map and Guide to Golden Gate Park*. It costs $2.25 and is available at the museum bookshops in the park.

Phone: (415) 666-7200 (general park information).
Hours: The park is open for sightseeing from sunrise to sunset. Parking is not allowed in the park between 10 p.m. and 5 a.m.
Admission: Free. The three museums, the Conservatory of Flowers, and the Japanese Tea Garden charge admission fees.
Parking: Free.
Restrooms: Yes. All the major buildings and playgrounds have restrooms.
Wheelchair Access: Much of the park is accessible.

Golden Gate Park — Western Half

The western half of Golden Gate Park extends from Cross-Over Drive to the Great Highway at the ocean.

The western half of the park offers more in the way of sports activities, and it has more lakes and more open space.

Almost dead center in the park, just north of JFK Drive, is Lloyd Lake. Standing next to it is a portico of six Ionic columns, known as **Portals of the Past**. This stone doorway was the only surviving portion of a Nob Hill mansion that was destroyed in 1906. It was moved to the lake in 1909.

Head west on JFK Drive. Off to the left, across from 30th Avenue, is **Lindley Meadow**, a broad expanse of green lawn sheltered by eucalyptus and cypress trees. It's a great place for picnics, frisbee throwing, and the like.

Just across JFK Drive from the west end of Lindley Meadow is **Spreckels Lake**. This picturesque lake is the second largest in the park. It is also one of the few lakes that has benches all around it. The south side of the lake is reserved from 10 a.m. to 1 p.m. daily for model boaters. It's fun to watch these miniature vessels zip along the surface, their operators guiding them by remote control.

Across from Spreckels Lake, at the intersection of JFK Drive and 36th Avenue, are the **Golden Gate Park Stables**. They offer one-hour guided trail rides for individuals and groups through the park's meadows and woodlands.

South of the stables is the giant outdoor **Golden Gate Park Stadium,** also known as the **Polo Field,** because in the early 1900s local aristocrats used this as their private polo field. Today the stadium is used for amateur rugby and soccer matches, football practice, jogging, and local track and field events.

Just farther west on JFK Drive on the right is the **Buffalo Paddock**. Buffalo have "roamed" in this large enclosure since the 1890s, although the current group was acquired in 1984 from a herd in Wyoming. Placid as cows, they mainly congregate near the feeding trough, where they munch on hay and alfalfa.

Continuing west on JFK you will next cross over **Chain of Lakes** Drive East, so named for the chain of three lakes that it passes. North and Middle lakes have footpaths around them while South Lake, the smallest of the three, does not.

Finishing up on JFK Drive as it curves to the right, you will be passing the **Golden Gate Park Golf Course**. The entrance to the parking lot is just to the right after you turn on 47th Avenue. The nine-hole, par three course is open to the public daily.

In the northwest corner of the park, in sight of the Pacific Ocean, is the **Dutch Windmill**. It was built in 1902, and until the 1930s helped supply part of the park's water supply by tapping into an underground stream. Eventually the windmill fell into disrepair as other water sources came into use. It was restored in 1981, but no longer pumps water. Next to the windmill is the **Queen Wilhelmina Tulip Garden**. Every April thousands of tulips burst into bloom in this small but elegant garden.

In the southwest corner of the park is another windmill, the **Murphy Windmill**. It was built in 1905 as a companion to its northern neighbor. Like the Dutch Windmill it too fell into decay. But it has not been restored, and its wooden sails lie rotting on the ground next to it.

From the Murphy Windmill, Martin Luther King Jr. Drive takes you east back into the park. Where it forks with Middle Drive West, following either will take you near three lakes. If you stay on Middle Drive West you'll pass right by the prettiest of the three, **Metson Lake**, home to a family of ducks.

Just across the drive is a grassy knoll. If you look through the trees at its edge you'll see that you are at quite an elevation above the rest of the park. Down below to the left is the Stadium mentioned above, and to the right is **Speedway Meadow,** so named because during the Victorian era this greensward served as a "dragstrip" for horses and carriages.

Phone: (415) 668-7360 (Stables); (415) 751-8987 (Golf Course).
Admission: Both of the above charge varying fees.
Restrooms: Check the *Map and Guide to Golden Gate Park* .
Hours, Parking, and **Wheelchair Access:** See Golden Gate Park East.

Grand View Park

Located in San Francisco's Sunset district between 14th and 15th
avenues at Moraga Street.

This little-known and seldom-visited park is scarcely more
than a rocky knob, but it has what it claims: a grand view. From
the rocky crest at the summit there are sweeping views looking
north. On a clear day you can see the tall office buildings of San
Francisco's financial district, part of the East Bay, much of the bay
itself, Angel Island, Tiburon, the twin towers of the Golden Gate
Bridge, and the Marin headlands.

Short of being up in an aircraft, this is also the best overview
of Golden Gate Park, since you can see from the beginning of the
Panhandle to the windmills at the western edge of the park by the
ocean. On a really clear day you can see the Farallon Islands, 17
miles offshore.

This rocky outcropping is actually part of an ancient seabed
that is composed of diatoms, which are tiny, one-celled organisms. And the sand surrounding this rocky knob is the residue of
Sierra Nevada granite that was eroded by glaciers and washed to
the ocean.

This seemingly unpromising site for vegetation is also one of
the last habitats for two rare and endangered plants, the dune
tansy and the Franciscan wallflower. A descriptive board at the
west end of the summit has illustrations of both.

There are two sets of steps that lead to the park's summit. One
is on 15th Avenue at the eastern edge of the park and the other is
on 14th Avenue at the base of the southern rim.

Restrooms: No.
Wheelchair Access: No.

Japanese Tea Garden

Next to the Asian Art Museum in Golden Gate Park, San Francisco.

The Japanese Tea Garden is a sylvan retreat of delicate and exotic greenery. Stone paths and bridges meander past wooden pagodas, stone lanterns, and over ponds and streams and past a waterfall or two. It is a place to soothe the soul.

Nestled among the oriental magnolias, camellias, dwarf pines, and Japanese maples is a zen garden with its gently shaped bonsai trees; nearby sits a 9,000-pound bronze peace lantern, which was a gift from Japanese schoolchildren. Located in the center of the garden and towering above it is a multi-tiered pagoda that originally graced the Japanese pavilion at the 1915 Panama Pacific International Exhibition.

The Tea Garden's origin dates back to 1894 when it was part of the Midwinter Exposition held that year in Golden Gate Park. From then until 1942 it was run by a native Japanese, Makoto Hagiwara, and his descendants. Makoto created the fortune cookie, which he served at the Garden's teahouse. Unfortunately for him he neglected to patent his invention, and Chinese restaurateurs quickly claimed the cookie as their own.

If you have the time, stop in the teahouse for tea and a snack. If you sit along the front rail you'll have a nice view of the garden and you can watch koi swim lazily along in the pond below.

Phone: (415) 752-1171.
Hours: April through September, open daily 8:30 a.m. to 6:00 p.m.; October through March, open daily 9 a.m. to sunset.
Admission: Adults $2.00; Seniors (65+) $1.00; Children (6–12) $1.00.
Parking: You can park free on John F. Kennedy Drive and on other major roads in the park.
Restrooms: Yes.
Wheelchair Access: Partial.

Lafayette Park

Bordered by Gough, Sacramento, Laguna, and Washington streets in Pacific Heights, San Francisco.

Lafayette Park is a beautiful park of tall trees and broad, sloping green lawns. Like Alta Plaza, its neighbor to the west, it was laid out as a public park in the same 1855 survey of the Western Addition. It also occupies a choice hilltop location, but because of the vegetation and surrounding houses and apartment buildings the great views once available from it are now mostly obscured.

The park has an interesting history, much of it involving lengthy litigation with a squatter named Samuel Holladay who illegally built a house at the park's summit in the 1860s. It wasn't until 1936 that the house was finally torn down. In the meantime a multistory apartment building at the park's eastern edge had gone up (1925 Gough Street), where it remains today — a rare example of a private building in a public park.

Lafayette Park was a largely barren sandhill until the late 1890s, when greenery was finally planted. Most of the tall trees are located in the eastern half of the park. A flat, circular lawn at the summit — the highest point in Pacific Heights, at 378 feet — surrounded by a stand of mainly eucalyptus trees, marks the site of Holladay's house.

The park today is a popular spot for sunbathers and as a place for neighborhood residents to walk their dogs. There are two tennis courts and a fence-enclosed childrens playground. There are green wooden benches scattered throughout the park.

Restrooms: Yes (near the children's playground), but the doors are usually locked.
Wheelchair Access: Limited. Best points of entry would be at the intersection of Laguna and Clay or at the Washington Street entrance near Octavia Street, but there are no sidewalk cutouts to facilitate access.

Lake Merced and Fort Funston

Lake Merced is reached via Harding Road, which is near the intersection of Skyline Boulevard and the Great Highway in the southwest corner of San Francisco.

Lake Merced provides the only joint recreational facility for both fishermen and boaters within the San Francisco city limits. It is actually two large lakes, North Lake and South Lake. Both offer fishing for trout, bass, carp, and catfish. You can rent fishing tackle or bring your own. Boats for rent include rowboats, canoes, pedal boats, and electric motorboats.

For those not interested in water sports, grassy areas near North Lake are set aside as volleyball and picnic spots. Note that there is no wading or swimming allowed at Lake Merced.

Farther back in the park is Harding Park Golf Course. It has two nine-hole golf courses and is open to the public.

A little farther south, on the other side of Skyline Boulevard and occupying a bluff above the beach, is **Fort Funston**, a former U.S. Army post. Now part of the Golden Gate National Recreation Area, the main attractions are the numerous hiking trails through the sand dunes that provide great views of the Pacific Ocean and parts of San Francisco.

Another highlight is the chance to see hang-gliders up close. Because of the steep ridge on which Fort Funston sits and the steady winds that blow, particularly between March and October, this is a premier hang-gliding spot. Their "launch pad" is conviently located just below a wooden viewing deck at the end of the parking lot.

Phone: for Lake Merced only, (415) 753-1101.
Hours: Open daily, roughly sunrise to sunset.
Admission: Free. There are various charges at Lake Merced for fishing, boating, and golf.
Parking: Free.
Restrooms: Yes.
Wheelchair Access: Yes.

Mt. Davidson

Located in the south central part of San Francisco, southwest of Twin
Peaks and Diamond Heights.

Mt. Davidson is best noted for the sunrise services held every
Easter at the base of the giant concrete and steel cross at this
peak's summit. The cross is 103 feet high (it was supposed to be
only 100 feet, but there was extra concrete left over), dates from
1934, and is the fifth one that has stood on the site since 1923. All
of the previous crosses were of wood, but they didn't last long.
Several were turned into flaming torches by arsonists.

This hill, which is the highest in San Francisco at 938 feet, was
first surveyed by George Davidson in 1852. Davidson was a pioneer government surveyor who mapped much of the Pacific
Coast. He named the peak Blue Mountain, but in 1911 the name
was changed to honor Davidson.

As parks go it is not a very pretty one. The ground cover is
thick with ivy and thorny brambles; except for the trails to the
summit it affords little in the way of hiking or recreation. And the
fully grown eucalyptus and pine trees arrayed in a dense stand on
the western slope and on most of the summit completely block
what would be a spectacular view of the Pacific Ocean and the
coast.

The eastern slope is unforested, and provides a nice view of the
eastern half of the city and of the bay and the East Bay hills
beyond.

Directions: Trails to the summit start from Dalewood Way
and from Juanita Way.
Restrooms: No.
Wheelchair Access: No.

Mt. Diablo

In the East Bay hills above Danville in Contra Costa County.

Rising to a height of 3,849 feet, Mt. Diablo is the dominant geographic feature of the East Bay skyline.

Most visitors head straight to the summit to see the panoramic 360-degree view it affords. On clear days — the best ones are right after a winter storm — you can see San Francisco, the Golden Gate Bridge, and the Farallon Islands to the west, the James Lick Observatory on Mt. Hamilton to the south, Mt. Lassen to the north, and the peaks of the Sierra Nevada 140 miles to the east.

Crowning the summit is a stone tower built in the 1930s by the Civilian Conservation Corps. The interior has recently been converted into an attractive museum. The museum's exhibits focus on the region's geologic history, the Native Americans who inhabited the area, and on the park's varied habitats. The latter range from riparian woodland at the base of the mountain to arid rocky crests near the top.

The park has miles of trails for hikers, mountain bikers, and horseback riders. The fire roads and hiking trails allow one to explore the varied habitats and to watch for wildlife.

Mt. Diablo also has over 50 picnic sites. A good number of them are situated on bluffs where you can enjoy views while you dine alfresco.

Directions: From 680 take the Diablo Road exit. Follow Diablo Road to Mount Diablo Scenic Boulevard and turn left into the park.
From Walnut Creek the North Gate Road leads into the park.
Phone: (510) 837-2525.
Hours: The park is open daily 8 a.m. to sunset. The museum is open 11 a.m. to 5 p.m. weekends only.
Admission: $5.00 per vehicle, $1.00 per dog.
Parking: Free.
Restrooms: Yes.
Wheelchair Access: Yes for the museum and the immediate summit, no for the park trails.

Mt. Tamalpais State Park

Located in western Marin County off Highway 1.

To stand on the summit of Mt. Tamalpais on a clear day is to feel like a god on Mt. Olympus. The view is utterly spectacular. San Francisco Bay, and indeed much of northern California, is spread out before you. Far below are Mill Valley, San Rafael, and the other towns of the Bay Area — all inhabited by mere mortals.

Besides inhaling the rarefied air and the view from East Peak — as the summit is officially known — there is much more to see in this large and beautiful park. If you love hiking, or even just walking, "Mount Tam" has a virtually inexhaustible supply of trails. Within the park proper there are 50 miles of trails, which in turn connect to over 200 miles of trails on adjoining land.

In addition to the views there is the opportunity to see the wildlife and the varied terrain to be found in the park: everything from evergreen forest and redwoods to wildflower-strewn meadows to rolling, grassy hilltops.

For further information and to obtain maps, visit the Pantoll Ranger Station Park Headquarters. It is located on the Panoramic Highway about five miles from the intersection of Highway 1 and Almonte Boulevard in Mill Valley.

After a day of hiking, a good way to unwind is to stop at the Mountain Home Inn, a rustic lodge with a restaurant and bar and an outdoor deck overlooking eastern Marin County and part of the bay. It is located on the Panoramic Highway about three miles east of the Pantoll station.

Directions: From U.S. 101 take the Highway 1 exit and follow the signs.
Phone: (415) 388-2070.
Hours: The park is open from sunrise to about one-half hour after sunset.
Admission and **Parking:** The park itself is free but the major parking lots, Pantoll, Bootjack, and East Park, all charge $5.00 per vehicle. The lot across from Mountain Home Inn and the lot at Rock Springs are free.
Wheelchair Access: The Verna Dunshee trail, which circles East Peak, is paved and is accessible part of the way.

Muir Woods National Monument

Located 12 miles north of San Francisco via U.S. 101 and State Route 1.

Muir Woods is home to the Bay Area's only large, intact stand of ancient redwoods. Here you will find the coastal redwoods, *Sequoia sempervirens*, the tallest living things in the world. The world record holder (367 feet) is located farther up the coast, but here you will see some in the 250-foot range — still mighty impressive.

Most people start their tour of Muir Woods at the visitor center at the end of the parking lot. A paved nature trail winds along the forest floor. Available at the visitor center is a free brochure with some basic information, but greater descriptive detail can be found in the Muir Woods Guide to the Park Trails brochure, which costs a dollar. This, or the free trail guide (please recycle after use) provide the key to the numbers on plaques you will see posted near trees along the paved path.

Redwood Creek, a stream that meanders along the forest floor past the biggest trees, is home to crayfish, salamanders, fingerling steelhead trout, and silver salmon, which spawn there during the winter. Among the plants, note the mushrooms, ferntail, and large ferns thriving under the perpetual shade the trees provide.

For the more adventuresome, a number of trails branch off the paved loop and climb through the vegetation into parts of the surrounding Tamalpais State Park. Here the crowds thin out and you will be able to enjoy the silence of the forest at a graceful remove from the noises of civilization. You will also stand a better chance of seeing some of the animals — such as deer, foxes, and raccoons — who themselves prefer to avoid the crowd.

Phone: (415) 388-2595.
Hours: Open daily 8:00 a.m. to sunset.
Admission: Free. Visitor center, gift shop, and snack shop.
Parking: Free.
Restrooms: Yes.
Wheelchair Access: Yes.

Olompali State Historic Park

Located two and a half miles north of Novato on the west side of
Highway 101 in Marin County.

California history buffs will enjoy visiting this little-known
park. Here you will find physical remnants from the time of the
Indians to the Mexican era to that of the white settlers who arrived in the wake of the gold rush.

Olompali was the site of one of the largest and most important
Coast Miwok villages in Marin County; it existed from 2000 B.C
until the mid-19th century. Indians from this village may have
been some of those who greeted Sir Francis Drake during his stay
on the Marin County coast in 1579. Indeed, an Elizabethan six-
pence was reportedly found here during archeological excavations during the 1970s.

The only vestige left from the time of the Native Americans,
however, is what is known as the "kitchen rock," a large stone
with mortar holes bored into it, which the Indians used for grinding acorns and seeds.

Structures survive from later periods — the ruins of an 1830s
adobe house and wood-frame ranch buildings dating from the
1850s to the 1880s, including two barns that were in use continu-
ously until the 1970s.

Further details on Olompali's history are provided in a self-
guided tour brochure available as you enter the park. For those
interested in more traditional park activities the park offers hiking trails and picnic tables.

Phone: (415) 892-3383.
Directions: If northbound on Highway 101 look for the brown and yellow
Olompali State Historic Park sign on the west side of the highway. Go two
miles to San Antonio Road and make a U-turn.
Hours: Open daily 10 a.m. to 7 p.m.
Admission: $2.00 per vehicle, $1.00 per dog.
Restrooms: Yes.
Wheelchair Access: Yes.

Point Reyes National Seashore

Located 25 miles northwest of San Francisco in western Marin County. The park entrance is on Bear Valley Road, which turns west from Highway 1 just north of Olema.

San Francisco is perhaps the only major city in the U.S. that can boast a 32,000-acre oceanfront park practically at its doorstep. Located a short drive north of San Francisco, Point Reyes is a largely unspoiled wilderness of beaches, sand dunes, estuaries, bays, inlets, and forests.

Start at the Bear Valley Visitor Center, where you can pick up a park map that shows all of the park's roads and trails, and pinpoints places of interest. The visitor center also has attractive exhibits on the area's history and flora and fauna.

Near the visitor center are the Kule Loklo Village and the earthquake trail. Kule Loklo is a reconstruction of a Miwok Indian village. The 0.6-mile earthquake trail takes you directly over the San Andreas fault. Here you can see a relic of the 1906 earthquake: a fence that crossed the fault is now two fences offset by 16 feet.

Drakes Bay is so named because Sir Francis Drake is believed to have stopped here in 1579 during his voyage around the world. The Kenneth C. Patrick Visitor Center at Drakes Beach can provide more information on Drake and his possible landing spot.

Also of historic interest is the 1870 lighthouse at the park's southern tip. The lighthouse is open most days, but even when it isn't, on clear days you'll be treated to spectacular views of the cliffs, the beach below, and the ocean.

Phone: (415) 663-1092.
Hours: The park itself is open from sunrise to sunset. The Bear Valley Visitor Center is open daily 9 a.m. to 5 p.m. The Kenneth C. Patrick Visitor Center is open weekends and holidays only, 10 a.m. to 5 p.m.
Admission: Free.
Parking: Free.
Restrooms: Yes.
Wheelchair Access: Yes for the earthquake trail and the visitor centers.

Portsmouth Square

In downtown San Francisco, bounded by the following streets — Clay, Kearny, Washington, and Walter U. Lum Place.

Portsmouth Square was the heart of early San Francisco.

Laid out as a plaza in 1839 by the Mexican authorities as part of the town's first street plan, it served as the nascent city's social and business center. At that time the shoreline of San Francisco Bay was only a block to the east — about where Montgomery Street is today. Goods were unloaded from ships and brought to the adobe custom house on the plaza's northwest corner.

The plaza received its name in 1846 when California became part of the United States during the war with Mexico. On July 9 of that year the U.S. warship *Portsmouth* anchored at Yerba Buena Cove, and a troop of sailors and marines under the command of Captain John B. Montgomery (for whom Montgomery Street is named) raised the stars and stripes on the northwest corner of the plaza. A plaque near the flagpole marks the spot.

During the gold rush, Portsmouth Square was the center of action; saloons and gambling halls sprang up around the square. But as the nearby cove was filled in, business and commerce moved east and south; Chinese began to move into the area.

Today this small park serves as a much-needed open space for densely packed Chinatown. On sunny days the park is crowded with people from the neighborhood — the men in particular gather to play checkers and gossip. A children's playground serves the younger generation.

The park is currently undergoing a renovation. New restrooms were recently added. Future improvements include the addition of new seating and landscaping, and a new play area for tots.

Parking: There is a parking garage under the square. Enter from Kearny Street via a left turn from one-way Clay Street.
Restrooms: Yes.
Wheelchair Access: Yes.

The Presidio

The Presidio covers 1,480 acres in the northwest corner of San Francisco.

The Presidio is one of the more scenic spots in San Francisco. It offers superb vistas of the ocean, the Golden Gate Bridge, and San Francisco Bay, from a setting amid an expanse of greenery.

This historic military post, founded by the Spanish in 1776, is in the process of being converted into a national park. (But it is fully open to the public.)

With hundreds of military buildings on the grounds, many of them dating back as far as the 1860s, this will truly be a unique national park. The Presidio's master conversion plan calls for some of the more recent structures to be leased to organizations devoted to the study of social, economic, and environmental problems. The rest of the park, which has lots of open space, will be devoted to typical national park activities — sightseeing, hiking, biking, picnicking, camping, and the like.

All of the Presidio's current major attractions will stay pretty much as they are. Highlights include:

The **Main Post** and **Parade Ground**. Any tour of the Presidio should start here, since this is not only where the original Spanish fortification stood — look for the stone marker at the eastern edge of Pershing Square — but it also contains many historic buildings. Notable is the lineup of brick infantry barrracks along Montgomery Avenue on the west side of the parade ground, which were built between 1895 and 1897, and the fine row of officers' housing along Funston Avenue, which date from 1862. Also worth a visit is the **Presidio Museum** (see p. 26).

Due west of the parade ground is the **National Military Cemetery**. Burials of military personnel here date back as far as 1852. From this hillside cemetery there are beautiful views of the Golden Gate Bridge and the bay.

On the Presidio's northern shoreline is **Crissy Field**. Now mainly just an expanse of pavement, in the 1920s and early 1930s it was a military airfield. Several of the hangars that once housed wire and canvas biplanes stand at the western end of the field.

Just the other side of the steel fence is the **Golden Gate Promenade**, a walking, hiking, and jogging trail. A mile and a half in length, it extends from the St. Francis Yacht Club at the Presidio's northeast corner to **Fort Point** (see p. 54), under the Golden Gate Bridge. The best access is from either end, or at Crissy Field you can join the path near the Old Coast Guard Station.

The **Coastal Defense Batteries** just west of the Golden Gate Bridge toll plaza offer not just the chance to explore the concrete shells of some turn-of-the-century large gun emplacements, but also afford some picture-perfect views of the bridge itself and of the entrance to San Francisco Bay. The Coastal Trail starts from the toll plaza parking lot and winds under the bridge. It extends from the four batteries down to **Baker Beach** at the Presidio's southern end, a mile distant. Baker Beach offers sunbathing along a large strip of white sandy beach. There are also picnic tables nestled among the pine and cypress trees just east of the parking lots.

If you prefer to stick to your car, Lincoln Boulevard parallels much of the Coastal Trail. There are several turnouts along the way, the most popular one (especially at sunset) is located at the intersection with Washington Boulevard.

Access: The main entrance is from Lombard Street at the park's eastern border. Crissy Field can best be reached by the entrance at the end of Marina Boulevard. Along the southern border there is access via Presidio, Arguello, and Lincoln boulevards. Coming from Marin County take a right immediately after exiting the toll plaza.
Phone: Presidio Resource Center, (415) 556-1874.
Hours: The Presidio is accessible at all hours. The Presidio Resource Center at Building 102 at the western edge of the parade ground is open daily 10 a.m. to 3 p.m.
Admission: Free.
Parking: There are paved lots in the Main Post area on the parade ground and across from the Presidio Museum. Crissy Field has plenty of parking. At the Coastal Defense Batteries there is a dirt lot in front of them near the toll plaza. More parking is available just south, off Langdon Street.
Restrooms: Yes.
Wheelchair Access: Call the Resource Center number above for accessibility for specific locations.

Sibley Volcanic Regional Preserve

In the Oakland hills just south of the Caldecott Tunnel.

Few Bay Area residents and even fewer visitors realize that underlying the hills above Berkeley and Oakland are the remnants of four volcanoes. Sibley Volcanic Regional Preserve has self-guiding trails that let you explore a portion of one of them — called Round Top — and learn something about this little known aspect of Bay Area geology.

Some nine to ten million years ago the East Bay hills were alive with volcanic activity. Convulsions from deep in the earth caused uplift that led to the Round Top volcano being tilted on its side. Subsequent erosion and modern day road cuts and quarrying have exposed cross sections of this long extinct volcano.

Pick up a brochure at the visitor center before starting out. It has a map and nine numbered paragraphs that correspond to numbered posts in front of notable rock formations. The information will help explain what you are seeing.

Round Top does not much resemble a Hawaiian volcano; it is much more ancient, and because it was tilted on its side it lacks the usual crater. Nevertheless, embedded in the hillsides you can see distinct lava flows, volcanic ash, and red-baked cinders.

If you visit on a clear day you will also be treated to superb views. To the east is Mt. Diablo, and to the west is the bay, San Francisco, and the Farallon Islands far out in the Pacific Ocean.

Directions: From Highway 24 take Fish Ranch Road exit east of Caldecott Tunnel. Go 0.8 mile to Grizzly Peak Blvd.; turn left and go 2.4 miles on Grizzly to Skyline Blvd. Turn left on Skyline into the park entrance.
Phone: (510) 562-7275 (regional headquarters).
Hours: Daily 8 a.m. to 6 p.m. (may close early due to darkness or weather.)
Admission: Free.
Parking: Free.
Restrooms: Yes.
Wheelchair Access: The visitor center and a 300-yard-long paved trail to the left of it are accessible.

Stern Grove

Sloat Boulevard and 19th Avenue, San Francisco.

Stern Grove is best known for its Midsummer Music Festival. Every Sunday at 2 p.m. from mid-June to mid-August the Grove hosts a free outdoor concert. The park is named for Sigmund Stern, a nephew of pioneer jeans maker Levi Strauss and one of the inheritors of Strauss's $6 million estate when he died in 1902.

The concerts provide a great opportunity to enjoy performances by local and visiting talent in the fields of classical music, ballet, opera, and jazz. The San Francisco Symphony, the San Francisco Ballet, international opera stars, and the Preservation Hall Jazz Band from New Orleans usually make appearances each year. Bring a blanket, a picnic hamper, and some warm clothes — it can be foggy and windy here during the summer — and find your own little patch of green on the lawn.

Nearby are picnic tables and a barbecue pit. And for those who feel like some exercise there are hiking trails that wind through the eucalyptus and fir trees behind the embankment facing the stage.

Stern Grove is, in a way, two parks. The concert and picnic area lie in a hollow below street level. But just beyond the main entrance — extending west down Sloat Boulevard and hidden behind shrubbery — is a flat stretch of land that holds a children's playground, a putting green, two tennis courts, and sixteen horseshoe pits.

Phone: (415) 398-6551 (for Midsummer Music Festival).
Parking: There is a free parking lot with a limited number of spaces. The entrance is on Sloat Boulevard just west of 19th Avenue.
Restrooms: Yes.
Wheelchair Access: Yes.

Strybing Arboretum and Botanical Garden

In Golden Gate Park near 9th Avenue, San Francisco.

Strybing Arboreteum is a garden of earthly delights. Covering 70 acres in Golden Gate Park, it is home to over 7,500 plants from all over the world.

Plants are grouped either by country or are arranged in thematic sections. Horticultural examples from Pacific Rim countries predominate, however, so there is good representation from Australia, New Zealand, Chile, Japan, and other Asian nations.

The native California plants section is the largest. Here you will find bunch grasses, manzanita, madrone and Coast Live Oak trees, and many others. You might also look for yerba buena, the mint-like ground cover for which San Francisco was first named.

Thematic sections include the Garden of Fragrance, which has plaques in braille for the visually impaired, and the Biblical Garden, which has plants mentioned in the Bible or that are known to have been growing in the Middle East at the time the Bible was written. Also of interest is the Moon Viewing Garden, a partial re-creation of the Katsura Imperial Gardens of Kyoto, Japan.

Broad paved paths wind throughout the arboreteum; gravel and dirt trails lead deeper into the foliage for the more adventuresome. Strybing is one of the few places in the state where you can go from a California grassland environment to a redwood grove to a desert-like succulent garden in just a few steps.

Phone: (415) 661-1316.
Hours: Open weekdays 8 a.m. to 4:30 p.m.;
weekends and holidays 10 a.m. to 5 p.m.
Admission: Free.
Parking: Free parking is available on Martin Luther King Jr. Drive, which skirts the arboreteum, or on Lincoln Way just outside the park.
Restrooms: Yes.
Wheelchair Access: Yes.

Sutro Heights Park, Sutro Baths Ruins, and the Cliff House

The entrance to Sutro Heights Park is at Point Lobos and 48th avenues. The Cliff House and the ruins of Sutro Baths are nearby.

All this oceanfront land once belonged to Adolph Sutro, a German immigrant who made his fortune on Nevada's Comstock Lode. In the 1890s Sutro built a lavish home (since demolished) in the park that is now named for him, amid manicured lawns and exotic plants and trees. The grounds were studded with copies of Greek and Roman statuary, a few of which still exist.

Be sure to visit the parapet, the crenelated stone semi-circle at the summit. On all but the most fog-bound days there are magnificent views from here looking south down Ocean Beach and looking north along the Marin County coast.

Directly below the parapet, on the other side of Point Lobos Avenue, is the Cliff House. In 1896 Sutro built a spectacular German chateau on this site — the third of five Cliff Houses. It burned in 1907. Today's nondescript version houses several restaurants, a bar, a deli, and a gift shop.

On the view deck below street level at the Cliff House are the Musée Mécanique (see p. 16) and a visitor center, where you can obtain books and further information. From here you can see **Seal Rocks,** home to various birds and to sea lions — but not to seals.

Upstairs, from the sidewalk along Point Lobos Avenue, you can see the ruins of **Sutro Baths**. Only the foundations remain of what was a mammoth public swimming emporium. It had seven swimming pools and could accomodate up to 25,000 people.

Phone: Visitor Center, (415) 556-8642.
Admission: Free.
Parking: Plenty of free parking nearby.
Restrooms: Yes, in the Cliff House area.
Wheelchair Access: Yes for the Cliff House and most of Sutro Heights Park. No for Sutro Baths ruins.

Tilden Regional Park

The park occupies the entire ridge along the Berkeley hills.

This 2,000-acre park has served the recreational needs of East Bay and Bay Area residents since the 1930s. It has something for everyone — picnic areas, trails open to hikers, cyclists, and horseback riders, a swimming hole, a botanic garden, rides for children, an educational center, even a golf course.

There are helpful maps of the park posted on information boards at the park's various entrances. You can pick up your own copy at the botanic garden's visitor center. The lovely botanic garden, by the way, provides the opportunity to see what California looked like before white settlers arrived, because it is devoted solely to native California plants.

There are numerous picnic locations scattered throughout the park; each has sturdy wooden picnic tables and metal barbecue grills. On hot days Lake Anza, in the middle of the park, provides a cool, wet haven for swimmers.

Children will love riding the miniature steam train and the antique merry-go-round with its brightly painted wooden carousel animals. There is also a separate location for pony rides. Not far away is the Little Farm, where it's possible to hand feed barnyard animals. Next to the farmyard is the Environmental Educational Center, which has on exhibit a miniature version of the Wildcat Creek watershed.

Directions: Follow the signs from Grizzly Peak Boulevard.
Phones: In the 510 area code they are as follows: District HQ, 562-7275; Botanic Garden, 841-8732; Merry-Go-Round, 524-6773; Train Ride, 548-6100; Pony Ride, 527-0421; EEC, 525-2233.
Hours: The park is open daily sunrise to sunset; call the above attractions for their days and hours.
Admission: The park itself is free; there are nominal charges for the rides and for Lake Anza.
Parking: Free.
Restrooms: Yes.
Wheelchair Access: Yes except for the dirt hiking trails.

Twin Peaks

Located virtually in the geographic center of San Francisco, just north
of Diamond Heights.

Twin Peaks' prime attraction is the panoramic view it offers.
Just shy of being the highest point in The City, the peaks offer a
lofty promontory from which to see San Francisco spread out
before you.

The main viewing area (and parking area) is actually a shorter
knob just to the north of the peaks. For the more adventuresome
there are trails to the top of the peaks themselves.

During the day you can see a panorama of The City and the
bay, extending from the Golden Gate Bridge to the north to the
San Mateo Bridge to the southeast. At night the view is equally
spectacular but in a different way, since what you see then are the
glittering lights of San Francisco and the bay's shoreline cities.

This dual-mounded hilltop has been one of the more distinc-
tive geographic landmarks since the time of the Indians, who saw
the two peaks in a creation legend as a quarreling man and wife
who had been separated by the Great Spirit. The Spanish, with a
bit more imagination, christened the peaks "Los Pechos de la
Choca" — the Breasts of the Indian Maiden. The early Anglo
settlers gave it the more prosaic name of Twin Peaks.

Located among a cluster of hilltops, Twin Peaks differs from its
neighbors in that it is largely bare of vegetation. It thus resembles
its natural state more than nearby Mt. Davidson and Mt. Sutro,
both of which are heavily forested with eucalyptus and other
non-native trees and plants.

Access: Twin Peaks Boulevard, a public street, from the north or
south is the only access. It winds around both peaks.
Parking: Parking spaces line a smaller peak north of Twin Peaks.
There also is a small parking lot.
Admission: There is no charge, and parking is free.
Restrooms: No.
Wheelchair Access: Yes for the viewing area, no for the trails to the peaks.

University of California Botanical Garden

Centennial Drive (in the hills above the U.C. stadium), Berkeley.

The U.C. Botanical Garden provides an around-the-world tour of botanical delights. Spread over its 33 acres are rare and beautiful plants from all over the world. It's a gardener's paradise, showing off nature in all its tremendous variety.

If you thought that succulents, for example, just meant cacti and ice plant, you'll be in for a surprise when you check out the Desert and Rain Forest House and see tables of them in a variety of shapes, some adorned with sharp needles, some with hair-like fuzz, and others bald and shiny smooth.

The California native plants section is a highlight. The state has such a diverse range of climates, environments, and soils, that it boasts a rich array of flora, some species of which are found nowhere else on earth. Informative boards stationed along the trails in this section and the others provide helpful details about the plants on view.

Many paths meander throughout the garden. Get off the main paved ones and onto the narrow dirt trails and you'll be more likely to discover some hidden treasures, such as the soothing stream that runs through the property. The garden is also a good place to bring a picnic lunch; there are several picnic tables. The California section has a cluster of them on a bluff surrounded by Coast Live Oak trees.

Phone: (510) 642-3343.
Hours: Open daily 9 a.m. to 4:45 p.m.
Admission: Free.
Parking: $0.75 per hour at the lot across from the garden's main entrance.
Restrooms: Yes.
Wheelchair Access: The paved paths but not the dirt trails can accommodate wheelchairs.

Washington Square

Bounded by Union, Stockton, Filbert, and Powell streets in San Francisco. Columbus Avenue cuts through its southwest corner.

This delightful park, in San Francisco's North Beach, is surrounded by green-painted, wooden benches, making it ideal for people-watching. It draws a wide mix of people. You might see elderly Italian men taking their ease, Chinese mothers playing with their young children, or San Franciscans of every stripe waiting at bus stops or wandering in and out of nearby cafes.

Its charm, in part, derives from its simple design and layout: a big patch of green lawn rimmed by trees and bushes, circled at its perimeter by a paved path that winds past the people-watching benches. A single monument occupies the west-central portion of the lawn — a statue of Benjamin Franklin. Donated to the park in 1879 by a teetotaler named Henry Cogswell, the now dry spigots at the statue's base once dispensed tap water to city residents.

The Franklin statue is the oldest piece of public sculpture in San Francisco, which is fitting because Washington Square, along with Portsmouth Square and Union Square, are the three oldest parks in The City, having been laid out as part of Jasper O'Farrell's 1847 survey. The park served as a tent city for refugees after the 1906 tragedy, since the fire consumed all of the surrounding buildings.

Today the park is bordered by a pleasant mix of commercial establishments, mainly restaurants and cafes, all of which contribute to Washington Square's people-friendly ambience. Saints Peter and Paul Roman Catholic Church, facing the park on the north, has served as the focus of North Beach's Italian Catholic community since it was dedicated in 1924.

Parking: Metered spaces abound but parking can be tight in this densely populated part of town.
Restrooms: No.
Wheelchair Access: Yes.

Family Attractions

PIER 39 is San Francisco's top attraction—and the second largest draw in the state after Disneyland.

Alcatraz

Located in San Francisco Bay north of Fisherman's Wharf.

Alcatraz Island, with its prison cellblocks that once housed Al Capone, "Machine Gun" Kelly, and Robert Stroud, "The Birdman of Alcatraz," is a unique and hugely popular attraction.

Alcatraz's history as a prison dates from the 1850s, but it is best known for the period 1934–1963 when it was the most infamous federal prison in the United States. Cellblocks A through D housed notorious gangsters and others deemed "incorrigble."

When you arrive at the dock (it is only a 10-minute boat ride from San Francisco) stop at the visitors center for an orientation. A free pamphlet is available, or you can spend anywhere from 50 cents on up for detailed maps and books. There is also a short movie about Alcatraz and its history.

To tour the island you may choose a ranger-led tour (there are several each day) or go on your own. The main advantage of a ranger-led tour is that the rangers provide more in the way of background and colorful anecdotes, such as how Al Capone would play his banjo in the empty shower room rather than take exercise with the other prisoners during recreation.

Several escape attempts were made from Alcatraz over the years. Probably the most famous one occurred in 1962 when three inmates surreptitiously hollowed out the area surrounding the air vents in their cells and made their way off the island. They were never seen again. You can see their cells in B Block and learn more about their daring escape.

Phone: (800) 229-2784. This is the number for the Red & White Fleet at Pier 41. Call for departure times and reservations.
Hours: The first boat departs about 9:45 a.m. and the last about 2:30 p.m.
Admission: Adults $8.75; Seniors (62+) $7.75; Children (5–11) $4.25. Prices are less if you do not choose the optional cellblock audio tour.
Parking: See the recommendations for Fisherman's Wharf and Pier 39.
Wheelchair Access: Yes for much of the island including the main floor of the cellblocks.

Bay Model

2100 Bridgeway (at Easterby), Sausalito.

This huge working model of the San Francisco Bay covers an acre and a half on the Sausalito waterfront. Water pumped through the model simulates the movement of tidal flows in San Francisco Bay. The model's purpose is to examine sediment deposits and changes in salinity, and it is also used for such things as predicting the effects of oil spills in the bay.

Before you enter the model you watch a short video — "The Bay Beneath" — which provides a lot of useful background information. One of the things you'll learn is that San Francisco Bay is not really a bay at all, but rather an estuary — a place where fresh and salt water mix.

The model is frequently dry. Since this is primarily a research facility (but fully open to the public), the water is pumped through the model on an irregular basis. Call ahead for the schedule. However, there is still plenty to see and learn when the model is "dry." In fact, it is more interesting that way, since you'll likely be surprised at just how shallow most of the bay really is.

Before you exit take a look at the excellent exhibit in the corner titled "Marinship." During World War II the Sausalito waterfront was home to a huge shipbuilding facility. The displays, videos, and artifacts here do a nice job of re-creating that era.

If you visit on a Saturday don't miss the opportunity to board the two historic ships out front — the *Wapama* and the tugboat *Hercules*. Both were used to haul lumber to San Francisco from the Pacific Northwest during the early part of this century.

Directions: Go down the ramp across from Easterby Street, straight ahead, and follow the brown and white signs.
Phone: (415) 332-3870 or 3871.
Hours: Tuesday - Saturday, 9 a.m. to 4 p.m.
Admission: Free.
Parking: Free lot next door. There is an additional lot behind the building.
Wheelchair Access: Yes.

Cable Cars

The cable cars run only in the northeast corner of San Francisco.
(See the map on page ix for the cable car routes.)

The cable cars are one of San Francisco's biggest draws — and, with the possible exception of the Golden Gate Bridge — symbolize San Francisco more than any other attraction.

A hundred years ago a dozen cable car lines served much of San Francisco, extending a total of 112 miles; a line even went out as far as the Cliff House at Lands End. Many cities then had cable car systems. Today, with three lines covering just 19 miles, San Francisco has the last remaining one.

The cable cars traverse some of the most visited and most scenic parts of town. The Mason-Taylor line passes Union Square, stops near Chinatown, and terminates at Bay Street near Fisherman's Wharf. The Powell-Hyde line passes the famous "crookedest" part of Lombard Street and turns around at Aquatic Park near Hyde Street Pier and the Cannery. The California Street line runs east-west through the financial district, up and down Nob Hill, and terminates at the Hyatt Regency on its eastern end and at Van Ness Avenue on its western end.

Cable cars operate by means of a "grip," which clamps onto a continuously-moving woven steel cable running beneath the street. When the grip is engaged the car moves at a maximum speed of 9½ miles an hour. When the grip is released, a brake is engaged and the car comes to a stop.

You can board cable cars at most intersections You can best be assured of a seat by waiting at one of the turnarounds, especially during the summer when cars are crowded.

Phone: (415) 673-MUNI.
Hours: Cars run daily from about 6 a.m. to 12:30 or 1 a.m. Signs at the embarkation point or at many intersections provide exact times.
Admission: Adults (18–64) $3.00; Children (5–17) $1.00; Seniors and Disabled $1.00. All-day passes good for unlimited rides cost $6.00.
Wheelchair Access: No.

Fisherman's Wharf

On San Francisco's north waterfront. The heart of the district is encompassed by the Embarcadero, and Powell, Beach, and Hyde streets.

Fisherman's Wharf is at the top of the list for many visitors to San Francisco. Up until the 1960s it was, as the name implies, primarily a commercial fish depot. Although remnants of it survive — dozens of fish trawlers still occupy berths along the waterfront — the area now is a retail mecca of stores and restaurants.

The core is the area surrounding Jefferson and Taylor streets. On the northwest corner of that intersection and extending down each side of the street are many sidewalk fish and chowder stalls where you can buy seafood cocktails, cracked crab, and sourdough bread. The south side of Jefferson Street between Taylor and Powell is lined with T-shirt and souvenir shops and such attractions as a wax museum, the Guinness Museum of World Records, and the Ripley's Believe It or Not Museum (see p. 27).

Across Jefferson at Pier 45 is the U.S.S. *Pampanito* (see p. 130). Piers 41 - 43½ house the the Red & White Fleet. They offer cruises of the bay and ferry service to Alcatraz (p. 118), Sausalito and Tiburon, Angel Island (p. 83), Muir Woods, (p. 103) and Marine World Africa USA (p. 128) in Vallejo. Just west of PIER 39 (p. 131) the Blue & Gold Fleet also offers cruises of the bay.

More restaurants and retail shops can be found at the nearby Anchorage Shopping Center and The Cannery, a former warehouse that has been converted into a shopping complex.

The Hyde Street Pier (see p. 124) is just a half a block away, and beyond it is beautiful Aquatic Park, a lovely greensward with fine views of the bay.

Parking: Parking is expensive in this area. There is a lot across from Jefferson Street and a multi-level garage across from Pier 39. The former charges $2.00 per hour, the latter $4.00 per hour. Many restaurants will validate, good for an hour or two.
Wheelchair Access: Yes, the Wharf area is all on level ground.

Ghirardelli Square

900 Northpoint Street (between Polk and Larkin), San Francisco.

This appealing complex of retail shops and restaurants is one of San Francisco's most popular tourist destinations. Ghirardelli Square's commercial brick buildings — the former Ghirardelli Chocolate Company — comprise an early, successful example of the adaptive reuse of abandoned factories.

There was talk of demolishing them, but fortunately for San Francisco, William Matson Roth, heir to a shipping fortune, purchased the site and started converting it to the festive marketplace it is today. It opened for business in 1964, and set a standard that has since been emulated by Quincy Market in Boston, South Street Seaport in New York, and other such adaptive reuse projects.

Today there are 63 specialty shops and 13 restaurants; most of the latter feature international cuisine. You can buy anything from inexpensive gimcracks to museum-quality art and collectibles, and you can allay your hunger in settings ranging from carryout food to expensive elegance. Retailers range from national names such as Ann Taylor, Benneton, and the Nature Company to one-of-a-kind shops.

Ghirardelli derives its charm not only from its renovation and such inspired touches as local sculptor Ruth Asawa's playful "Mermaid Fountain," but also from its singular ambience, which includes its multiple levels arrayed with attractive landscaping and its superb setting by the bay. All the restaurants, for example, have at least several tables with views of the water.

On weekends and during the summer, jugglers, musicians, and other performers entertain in the Square's public areas.

Hours: The retail stores are open 10 a.m. to 6 p.m. daily; till 9 p.m. during the summer.
Parking: There is an underground garage. Entrances are on Larkin and Beach streets. There are also free and metered spaces on nearby streets.
Wheelchair Access: Yes.

Great America

1 Great America Parkway, Santa Clara.

Known as Paramount's Great America since the movie/publishing conglomerate bought it in 1993, this 100-acre amusement park has plenty to offer thrill seekers. It is especially popular with teens and pre-teens.

Since Paramount has taken over, newer rides and attractions have been geared to various Paramount motion pictures. An example is the "Days of Thunder" experience based on the Tom Cruise movie about auto racing. While you are strapped in theater seats that dip and slant, a huge screen projects what it's like to be careening around a racetrack dodging other cars at 200 mph.

Rides at the park range from the mild to the wild, but the big deal here is the roller coaster rides. There are four major ones, most with scary names such as "The Grizzly," "Vortex," or "The Demon." The newest ride is "Top Gun." The twist to this one is that you ride *below* the rail so that as you hurtle through the loops and turns your feet are dangling in the air.

If "Top Gun" doesn't get your heart racing you might try "The Edge," in which you are strapped into a metal cage that is cranked to the top of a tall tower and then released in a free fall.

To take a break from the action, settle into a seat at the Pictorium Theater and see the movie *Blue Planet*. Shown on a 70-foot-high screen with startling clarity, you'll get to see the earth as the astronauts do as they circle the globe on the space shuttle.

Directions: From Highway 101 take the Great America Parkway exit. Head east toward the bay and follow the signs.
Phone: (408) 988-1776.
Hours: Open daily during the summer; weekends only in the spring and fall from 10 a.m. until between 7 p.m. and 11 p.m., varying by season.
Admission: General Admission (ages 7–54) $25.95; Seniors (55+) $18.95; Children (3–6) $12.95; Under 3, Free.
Parking: $5.00 per vehicle.
Wheelchair Access: Yes.

Hyde Street Pier

2905 Hyde Street (on the bay at the foot of Hyde Street), San Francisco.

The Hyde Street Pier has one of the finest collections of historic ships in the world. It offers the rare opportunity to board several of the few remaining 19th-century sailing ships in existence.

The crown jewel is the *Balclutha,* a three-masted square-rigger that was one of the last sailing ships built. Constructed in 1886, she made numerous trips around Cape Horn and up to Alaska carrying grain, coal, salmon, and other cargo. The ship played a bit part in the 1934 movie *Mutiny on the Bounty.* Be sure to go below deck to see the captain's cabin with its polished woods and Victorian-era furniture.

On the water just in front of the *Balclutha* is the *C. A. Thayer,* a former lumber schooner. This workaday windjammer graphically conveys how tough life at sea could be. Down below, in the dark underbelly of the ship, note the hard, wooden slat berths where the sailors and fishermen slept.

The large vessel on the other side of the pier is the *Eureka,* a steam-driven paddle-wheel ferryboat. From the 1920s to the 1950s the *Eureka* served on San Francisco Bay as a passenger and auto ferry. To re-create that era the lower deck contains some vintage autos of the 1920s and 1930s. The upper-level passenger deck, complete with a period piece newsstand, nicely conveys what commuting to San Francisco was like before the bay's two main bridges were built.

Phone: (415) 556-6435.
Hours: Open daily June to October, 10 a.m. to 6 p.m.; November to May, 10 a.m. to 5 p.m.
Admission: Adults (17–61) $3.00; Children (11–16) $1.00; Seniors, and Children (under 11) Free. The first Tuesday of the month is free to all.
Parking: Metered street parking, or try the garage underneath the nearby Cannery.
Wheelchair Access: Yes for the pier itself; partial access to the *Balclutha* and the *Eureka.*

Jack London Square

Jack London Square is located along the Oakland Inner Harbor
waterway between Embarcadero, Clay, and Alice streets.

Jack London Square is an eight-block strip of specialty shops
and restaurants occupying a stretch of the Oakland waterfront.

Named for the famous author, this outdoor mall comes by its
association with Jack London honestly. Although he was born in
San Francisco, London was raised in Oakland and as a boy spent
time along this very waterfront. In fact, there are two historic
buildings at the Square that are intimately associated with him.

Heinold's First and Last Chance Saloon, which has stood at
this location since 1880, was frequented by London throughout
his life. A photo on the wall across from the bar shows him at
about age 10 sitting at one of the saloon's tables reading a book.
These same tables are still there today. Heinold's, incidentally, is
the only business establishment in California that is known to still
use gas fixtures for indoor lighting.

The other historic structure is Jack London's Klondike cabin,
which stands just outside Heinold's. London lived in this cabin in
the wilds of Alaska in 1897 while prospecting for gold. The cabin
was located in 1968 and brought here for display.

If you haven't had enough of Jack London there also is a
museum devoted to him in the Jack London Village, a two-story
fortress of shops a few blocks to the south.

Besides the London memorabilia, the retail shops, and the
restaurants, there is a lovely wooden-plank promenade along the
water — a good place for a stroll after a meal.

Hours: Most of the shops and restaurants are open daily.
Admission: Free.
Parking: All the garages charge for parking, but the outdoor lot at Alice
and Embarcadero is free for the first three hours, $0.75 per hour thereafter.
Wheelchair Access: Yes, except getting into Heinold's might be tough due
to 1906 earthquake damage that tilted the floor.

S.S. *Jeremiah O'Brien*

On the north waterfront in San Francisco at Fort Mason, next to Pier 3.

A relic from World War II, the S.S. *Jeremiah O'Brien* is the last surviving, unaltered, and still operable Liberty ship of the more than 2,700 constructed. Liberty ships were cargo carriers; during the war they transported troops, food, ammunition, and other vital supplies to Allied battlefronts.

The *Jeremiah O'Brien* — named for the first U.S. naval hero of the Revolutionary War — was launched at Portland, Maine in 1943. During her three-year career she served first in the Atlantic — where she saw action in the Normandy campaign — and then was shifted to the Pacific, with San Francisco as her home port.

Today, with classical music playing on the ship's intercom instead of the sound of officers barking orders, you are free to roam the decks and peek into the various quarters. Of particular interest are the officers' quarters on the main deck near the bow. The *O'Brien's* skipper was the only one with his own shower and toilet, but even with these amenities note how spartan his quarters were.

Nearby are the chart room, the ship's hospital, the galley, and the mess room with its wooden rims around the tables to prevent dishes from sliding off. In the bowels of the ship is the labyrinthine engine room with its myriad pipes and staircases.

For children or the mechanically minded, there are several pieces of equipment that are still "operable". Foremost among them is the three-inch 50-caliber gun at the stern. By cranking wheels on the side you can raise and lower the cannon, or swivel it and train your sights on Alcatraz.

Phone: (415) 441-3101.
Hours: Open daily 9 a.m. to 3 p.m. except for major holidays.
Admission: Adults $2.00; Children under 13 $1.00; Seniors (65+) $1.00.
Parking: There is a free parking lot at Fort Mason Center.
Wheelchair Access: No.

Lombard ("Crookedest") Street

Located on the eastern slope of Russian Hill, it occupies the block between Hyde and Leavenworth streets.

This section of Lombard Street, dubbed "the crookedest street in the world," is one of San Francisco's most popular attractions.

During the summer tourist season the line of cars waiting to slowly slalom down this winding brick-paved thoroughfare can extend down the western slope of Russian Hill to Van Ness Avenue. Why this relatively banal thrill has proved so popular is hard to say, but the street's reputation is now firmly entrenched as an indelible part of San Francisco.

The street took on its present configuration in 1922 when a local druggist, who owned lots bordering this stretch, campaigned to have this once straight lane regraded into multiple twists and turns that would make the descent more gradual. The realignment changed the grade from a fairly steep 27 degrees to a more moderate 16 degrees. The resulting easier access did what its promoter hoped — it made the adjacent lots more valuable.

The street's descent starts at the intersection of Lombard and Hyde streets. The cityscape and bay views from here are spectacular. During the spring and summer the multi-colored puffball hydrangea plants that occupy the embankments between the roadway curves are in bloom, giving the site an added colorful dimension.

The Hyde Street cable car also stops here, providing a good way to see and photograph the scene for those who don't need to boast to their friends back home that they drove down "the crookedest street in the world."

Hours: Lombard Street is a public thoroughfare and as such is accessible 24 hours a day.
Admission: Free.
Parking: Free street parking but spaces nearby can be hard to find.
Wheelchair Access: No.

Marine World Africa USA

Marine World Parkway (off Highway 37), Vallejo. Vallejo is 30 miles
northeast of San Francisco.

Fun for the whole family, Marine World Africa USA offers a
wealth of wild animal attractions. Unlike zoos where the animals
placidly lie about, here they are paraded and kept active by train-
ers. In some cases you are allowed to pet or even feed the animals,
such as the giraffes; even small children may hand-feed them
apple slices or carrots.

Many of the attractions are organized around shows. A few of
the more popular ones are the whale and dolphin show featuring
giant killer whales in a large pool, the tiger and lion show, and the
monkey and chimpanzee show. You can pick up a schedule of
show times, and a park map, at the Clock Tower or Information
Center.

Permanent ongoing attractions include such things as the
aquarium, the "Shark Experience," and "Butterfly World," a
greenhouse you can wander through and examine up close dozens of species of butterflies flitting about.

Other entertainment (during the summer only) includes a high
speed water-ski and boat show, and what is billed as "the incred-
ible acrobats of China," whose amazing feats elicit crowd oohs
and aahs.

With so much going on, plan to spend a whole day here.

Phone: (707) 643-6722 for recorded information, otherwise (707) 644-4000.
Hours: Summer: Open daily, 9:30 a.m. to 6:30 p.m.;
Winter: Wednesday - Sunday, 9:30 a.m. to 5 p.m.
Admission: Adults $23.95; Seniors (60+) $19.95; Children (4–12) $16.95;
(3 and under, free);
Parking: $3.00 all day.
Wheelchair Access: Yes.

Oakland Zoo

9777 Golf Links Road (Golf Links Rd. exit from Interstate 580), Oakland.

In the early 1980s the Oakland Zoo was rated as one of the 10 worst zoos in the country. Happily, today things are different and the New Oakland Zoo, as it bills itself, has been revamped and vastly improved.

A major change has been to get animals out of confining individual cages and into open spaces that are re-creations of their natural habitats. Another is that enclosures have been designed to allow visitors to get as close to the animals as possible.

The changes are particularly evident with the elephants and lions. At the elephant enclosure you can stand at the rail next to a boulder-lined 60,000-gallon pool and watch Smokey, a giant African bull elephant, take his daily bath. The lions have been given a whole swatch of hillside to roam. The skyride tram in the park is a good way to see them, since it takes you up over their compound.

For kids there is a small, separate Children's Zoo. Here they can watch a playful sea otter go through its paces or, in keeping with the get-close-to-the-animals philosophy, they can hand-feed Scottish Highland cattle or pet the tame goats that wander freely in the yard.

While the Oakland Zoo lacks the pizazz of say Marine World Africa USA, the admission prices here are a real bargain by comparison.

Phone: (510) 632-9523.
Hours: Open daily 10 a.m. to 4 p.m. (weather permitting), 10 a.m. to 5 p.m. weekends, and daily during the summer.
Admission: Adults $4.50; Children (2–14) $3.00; Seniors (55+) $3.00.
Parking: $3.00 per vehicle.
Wheelchair Access: Yes.

U.S.S. *Pampanito*

Pier 45 at Fisherman's Wharf, San Francisco.

The U.S.S. *Pampanito* is the only World War II submarine on the West Coast and one of a handful still in existence.

After you board and adjust to the slight rocking of the boat in the water, note the four large gleaming brass torpedo tubes. The Japanese flags painted on them signify enemy ships sunk. Two huge torpedoes are securely strapped to the hull nearby.

The thing that strikes most first-time visitors to a submarine is how cramped it is. It's hard to believe that these narrow confines once were home to 10 officers and 70 enlisted men. Every inch of space was used; a prime example is the steel mesh bunks that were lashed to the hull during work hours and suspended by chains from the ceiling for sleeping.

The *Pampanito* was launched in 1943 and spent her two-year career in the Pacific, where she sank six Japanese ships, damaged four others, and rescued 73 Allied POWs.

When you leave the vessel (or before you board), check the panels at the entrance to the pier itself. Here you will find information about how hazardous submarine duty was, along with the grim statistics: out of 288 U.S. submarines launched during World War II, 52 — or almost one in five — never returned. The adjacent map pinpoints the last known location of some of these subs, which in navy parlance are "still on patrol."

Phone: (415) 441-5819.
Hours: Open daily 9 a.m. to 6 p.m.; to 9 p.m. during the summer.
Admission: Adults $4.00; Seniors and High School students $2.00; Children and military veterans $1.00.
Parking: Metered spaces abound in the Fisherman's Wharf area, but if you plan to stay a while there are parking lots across from Pier 45, at Pier 39, and at The Anchorage shopping center.
Wheelchair Access: No.

PIER 39

On the Embarcadero on San Francisco's northern waterfront.

Anchoring the east end of Fisherman's Wharf is San Francisco's biggest single tourist draw — PIER 39. The second most popular attraction in the state of California (after Disneyland), PIER 39 lures in excess of 10 million visitors a year.

The extra large pier, built on two levels, is home to over 100 shops selling a wide variety of gifts, apparel, jewelry, souvenirs, and toys and games. There are 10 full-service restaurants and a like number of fast-food takeout stands. Attractions include a carousel, an arcade with video, pinball, and other games, and a stage where mimes, magicians, and jugglers perform.

The most popular performers aren't on stage — they're lolling on floating docks off the west side of the pier. In January 1990 California sea lions — at first just a few but later hundreds — suddenly appeared and laid claim to these docks. Although most of these large, blubbery creatures lie sprawled sleepily in bunches, a few always put on a show by jostling for space, usually amidst a chorus of loud bellows.

Where to start with so many things going on? If you are new to San Francisco or a first time visitor to PIER 39 a good introduction to The City is the San Francisco Experience, located upstairs near the entrance. It is a 30-minute multi-media show employing slides, film, and sound effects to tell the story of San Francisco from the gold rush to the present. The lobby has a free exhibit on both the 1906 and 1989 earthquakes, supplemented by lots of dramatic photographs.

Phone: (415) 705-5500.
Hours: Open daily 10:30 a.m. to 8:30 p.m.; longer hours in the summer; shorter hours in the winter. Some businesses keep longer hours.
Admission: Free.
Parking: There is a multi-level garage across the street; rates are $4.00 hr., but restaurants will validate for up to two hours.
Wheelchair Access: Yes.

San Francisco Zoo

Located in the southwest corner of San Francisco at the intersection of
Sloat Boulevard and the Great Highway.

A day at the zoo is always a popular family outing, and despite
sometimes breezy or overcast conditions here by the ocean, the
park is able to sustain a wide variety of species. Like the Oakland
Zoo, the San Francisco Zoo is in the process of upgrading its
exhibits.

A recent and quite attractive new exhibit is the Primate Discovery Center. Large cages, which are more like aviaries, allow the
monkeys plenty of room to cavort. The ground level holds a
unique exhibit — a nocturnal gallery, where, in dim lighting
resembling moonlight, you can observe small primates, such as
the aptly-named Slow Loris, that only come out at night.

Big cats have always been a strength of the San Francisco Zoo.
Feeding time at the Lion House (daily at 2:00 p.m. except Mondays) is always a crowd pleaser. People press to the rail for a close
look at the sometimes snarling lions and tigers who are tossed
large hunks of meat that they quickly devour. Watching them eat
gives a real sense of the raw power of these "kings of the jungle."

For young children there is a separate Childrens Zoo within
the park. A highlight here is the barnyard, where children can pet
and hand-feed tame goats and other animals. Also found here, in
a separate building, is the Insect Zoo, where the emphasis is on
the dangerous and creepy. It offers a close look at scorpions,
spiders, tarantulas, and giant cockroaches — all securely behind
glass.

Phone: (415) 753-7083 (recorded information) or 753-7080.
Hours: Open daily 10:00 a.m. to 5 p.m.
Admission: Adults (16–64) $6.50 Seniors (65+) $3.00; Youth (12–15) $3.00;
Children (6–11) $1.00; Under 6, Free.
Parking: Free street parking on the south side of Sloat Boulevard.
Wheelchair Access: Yes.

Winchester Mystery House

525 South Winchester Boulevard (Winchester Boulevard exit, east off Highway 280), San Jose.

The Winchester Mystery House is the largest, and surely the strangest, house in California. Constructed between 1884 and 1922, this 160-room mansion was the work of Sarah Winchester, sole heir to the 20-million-dollar Winchester rifle fortune.

The eccentric Sarah, aggrieved by the loss of her husband and infant daughter, apparently was convinced that their premature deaths were caused by the spirits of those killed by Winchester rifles. Guided by a medium who decreed that only continuous construction at her San Jose estate would atone for those deaths and even delay her own demise, she embarked on an unparallelled building program that lasted until her death at age 82.

Sarah kept carpenters and craftsmen busy adding rooms to the house and sometimes tearing them down and remaking them as her whims dictated. Walking through the house today you will see doors that open onto blank walls; a staircase leading into a ceiling; and a window built into the floor. Whether these were simply mistakes or were attempts to ward off evil spirits — she was a lover of the occult — no one can say.

You may also wander the grounds on the self-guiding Garden Tour. The path takes you through the estate's gardens and past the foreman's house, the garage, the greenhouse, and other structures. In the courtyard is the Winchester Firearms Museum, which contains brace after brace of historic rifles (not just Winchesters).

Phone: (408) 247-2000.
Hours: Open daily from 9 a.m. Closing times range from 5 p.m. to 6:30 p.m. depending on the season. Tours depart every 10 to 15 minutes during summer and up to 30 to 45 minutes during winter.
Admission: Adults (13+) $12.50; Seniors (65+) $9.50; Children (6–12) $6.50.
Parking: Free.
Wheelchair Access: No for the house, yes for the grounds.

Fun for Children

The antique carousel at Golden Gate Park's Children's
Playground still provides thrills for youngsters.

Bay Area Discovery Museum

557 East Fort Baker (near the Golden Gate Bridge), Sausalito.

Spread among half a dozen former U.S. Army buildings at East Fort Baker in Sausalito is a "hands on" museum for young children — the Bay Area Discovery Museum. The guiding philosophy here is "play is the way children learn." To that end the exhibits are designed to encourage maximum interaction.

The museum is impressive in its scope and execution. Each building is organized around a particular theme: art, architecture and design, science, transportation, and other subjects.

One of the more popular attractions is the San Francisco Bay Room. Here children can crawl through an underwater sea tunnel, board a mockup of a boat and man fishing lines and reel in rubber fish, or they can pretend they are sidewalk vendors at The Grotto at Fisherman's Wharf and weigh ersatz crabs on a scale.

The newly constructed Discovery Hall houses changing exhibitions. Recent events have included one on the cuisine and cooking practices of foreign countries. It was followed by one on the ever-popular Muppets.

Most of the activities are designed for younger children, but the new Media Center for Electronic Arts is geared toward older kids as well. With instructors on hand to guide them they can practice on Apple Macintoshs that are stocked with various graphics programs.

Directions: From 101 heading north, cross the Golden Gate Bridge and take the Alexander Avenue exit; heading south take the last Sausalito exit, just before the bridge. Follow the signs to the museum.
Phone: (415) 332-9671.
Hours: Wednesday - Sunday, 10 a.m. to 5 p.m.; Tuesdays, the same hours during summer only.
Admission: $4.00 per person.
Parking: Free.
Age Range: 12 and under.
Wheelchair Access: Yes.

Children's Discovery Museum

180 Woz Way (at W. San Carlos), San Jose.

Open only since 1990 this new children's museum is the third largest of its kind in the U.S. It is designed to provide interactive learning in the arts, humanities, sciences, and technology. As such it has a wealth of buttons to push, handles to crank, and wands to wave.

Before kids get a chance to try out some of these hands-on wonders however, they are greeted near the entrance with some out-to-pasture vehicles they are free to explore. They can clamber around the deck of an American La France fire engine, walk through an ambulance, or climb aboard a Wells Fargo stagecoach.

The interactive exhibits are spread over two floors. One attention-getting demonstration on the first floor is called "Heartbeats." Here's a chance for them to use their bodies as musical instruments. By placing their hands on copper handprints they activate a drum that plays a rhythm based on their heartbeat. When they jump on a nearby trampoline, and try it again, the tune will change.

Nearby, an exhibit called "Drumbeat" lets kids experience what it's like to be an orchestra conductor. While a computer plays the notes to a song they select, they can wield the baton and by doing so control the tempo and the volume of the piece.

Upstairs in a darkened space is "Rhythms," a new project at the facility, where they can explore the use of strobes and lasers. Activating a strobe light over a moving chessboard, for example, makes the chess pieces seem to dance.

Phone: (408) 298-5437.
Hours: Tuesday - Saturday, 10 a.m. to 5 p.m.; Sunday, Noon to 5 p.m.
Admission: Adults $6.00; Seniors $3.00; Children (4–18) $3.00;
3 and under, Free.
Parking: The closest lot is across Woz Way.
Age Range: 3 to 13 years.
Wheelchair Access: Yes.

Children's Playground, Golden Gate Park

At the eastern end of Golden Gate Park just across from Kezar Stadium.

Opened in 1887, this is the oldest public children's playground in the United States. After more than a century of use (with several remodelings) it remains a popular spot.

The prime attraction here is the wonderful old-fashioned carousel. Accompanied by organ music, children and their parents can ride on gaily-painted lions, tigers, horses, giraffes, camels, and other animals. The carousel, which dates from 1913, has been here since 1941, when it arrived after being used at the Treasure Island world fair of 1939–40. It underwent a major restoration between 1977 and 1985.

Besides the carousel there is a variety of other things for kids to do. The main playground is a hive of activity. There are swings, slides, and a solid wooden treehouse structure for climbing.

There are also more traditional items, such as parallel bars, and rings attached to chains for swinging through the air. And there is a giant multi-colored plastic and metal geodesic jungle gym that is highly popular.

During the summer there are sometimes extra events, such as a Punch and Judy puppet show and a barnyard animal enclosure in which children can pet tame animals.

Hours: The playground is open daily. The carousel operates daily June 1 through September 30, 10 a.m. to 5 p.m. (last ride at 4:30 p.m.), and Thursday through Sunday only during the rest of the year from 10 a.m. to 4:00 p.m.
Admission: The playground is free. Carousel ride charges: Adults $1.00; Children $0.25; children under 39 inches tall free when accompanied by an adult.
Parking: Free parking lot off Bowling Green Drive.
Age Range: 10 and under.
Wheelchair Access: Yes.

Discovery Room - California Academy of Sciences

At the east end of the museum behind the Far Side Gallery.

Housed here is a roomful of objects, all of which are meant to be handled. The motto is "Please Touch."

The philosophy behind the Discovery Room is that rather than having a teacher or parent explain something in advance, children will learn on their own and at their own pace if they are left to discover things by themselves. Should they have questions, many of the objects have cards placed with them that supply answers, or they can ask the volunteer who is always in the room.

Some of the things they can touch and handle are a giant sponge, a queen conch shell, large pine cones, and various animal antlers and horns. They can also touch an actual giant dinosaur bone as well as a shark jaw, and feel the latter's sharp teeth.

Boxes on a shelf at the end of the room are organized by subject — fossils, reptiles and amphibians, shapes and shells, feathers, and so on. The one called "Build an Insect," for example, provides a velcro body onto which children can stick plastic wings. Photos in the box provide models to follow.

Many more things are found here, most of them nature oriented. Besides the inanimate objects mentioned there are also a few live animals one may watch. On view recently was a Pacific Coast newt; a separate enclosure held caterpillars and butterflies.

Phone: (415) 750-7155.
Hours: Tuesday - Friday, Noon to 4 p.m.; Saturday and Sunday, 10 a.m. to 4 p.m.
Admission: No extra charge beyond the regular museum admission fees.
Parking: Parking is free either in the concourse area in front of the museum or on Middle Drive East in back of it.
Age Range: 10 and under.
Wheelchair Access: Yes.

The Exploratorium

3601 Lyon Street (at the Palace of Fine Arts), San Francisco.

Tucked away in the far corner of the Palace of Fine Arts in a building the size of an airplane hangar is the Exploratorium, a delight for children of all ages and a veritable playground for the senses. With over 700 experiments and exhibits it's like visiting the workshop of some mad (albeit benign) scientist.

The museum's purpose is to increase interest in science through exploring natural phenomena. Virtually every experiment is hands-on — pushing buttons, twisting knobs, touching, feeling, handling, listening. Experiments run the gamut from simple displays of magnetism to those using holograms and lasers. A couple of the items to be found here are:

Golden Gate Bridge Video — By sitting at a color monitor and rolling a computer track-ball mouse you can "fly" over San Francisco and the Golden Gate Bridge; Going To Pieces — A black-and-white screen plays back your face and its motions. Then by pressing various buttons you can fracture and modify your face at varying speeds.

The premier exhibit at the Exploratorium is the geodesic Tactile Dome. It is totally dark inside. You walk, crawl, climb, slide, tumble, and otherwise make you way through, all the while feeling different objects and experiencing various textures. The Tactile Dome requires advance reservations.

Phone: (415) 563-7337. Tactile Dome, (415) 561-0362, call Monday - Friday between 2 p.m. and 4 p.m. for reservations.
Hours: Tuesday - Sunday, 10 a.m. to 5 p.m.; Wednesdays until 9:30 p.m. Closed Mondays except holidays.
Admission: Adults (18–64) $8.00; Youth (6–17) $4.00; Seniors (65+) $6.00; University Students $6.00; Disabled Persons $4.00; Children under 6, Free. Free for everyone the first Wednesday of the month.
Parking: There are parking spaces in front of and behind the Exploratorium or look for parking on nearby Baker Street.
Age Range: All ages.
Wheelchair Access: Yes.

The Jungle

555 Ninth Street (between Bryant and Brannan above Toys R Us), San Francisco.

This new indoor play facility is a madhouse of fun for children 14 and under.

The center of the room is occupied by a labyrinthine two- and three-level play structure made of brightly colored plastic tubes and white rope cargo nets. Kids can crawl and slide through the tubes, climb the cargo netting, and jump into pools filled with plastic balls.

On the perimeter are a game room with such carnival games as hoop shoot and skee ball, a snack bar with a seating area, and six separate birthday party rooms decorated with balloons, where kids celebrating birthdays can gather with their friends for cake and other goodies (the birthday rooms must be reserved in advance). There is also a separate play area for tots three and under, with play equipment geared to their level.

For parents who weary of the noise and frenzy there is a separate soundproof "Parents Only" room where it is possible to relax in comfortable chairs, read, watch TV, or sip cappuccino while the plentiful staffers keep an eye on things.

Phone: (415) 552-4386.
Hours: Monday, Noon to 7 p.m.; Tuesday - Thursday, 10 a.m. to 7 p.m.; Friday - Saturday, 9 a.m. to 9 p.m.; Sunday 10 a.m. to 7 p.m.
Admission: Each child is $5.95 for the first hour, $1.00 per hour thereafter; adults are free when accompanied by children.
Parking: Free lot; entrances are on Brannan and Bryant streets.
Age Range: 14 and under.
Wheelchair Access: Yes.

Lawrence Hall of Science

Centennial Drive, University of California, Berkeley.

Spread over two floors, the Lawrence Hall of Science has dozens of hands-on science experiments for children and adults. Perched high in the hills above the U.C. campus (on clear days the view from here is spectacular), this octagonal cement building is named after Nobel Prize laureate and former U.C. physics professor Ernest O. Lawrence.

To facilitate interaction and the learning process, many of the exhibits are manually operated. Pressing buttons, for example, can activate computers that talk to you. Pushing up or down on a lucite box filled with mineral oil and colored water demonstrates ocean wave action.

More elaborate exhibits include one titled "Where did the Polynesians Come From?" Pressing buttons in front of a large map of the Pacific Ocean enables you to sort through archeological and linguistic evidence to find the answer. Along the way you learn such things as how wind influences sailing a canoe.

The Planetarium offers changing shows on the heavens, the Biology Lab has small, tame animals that can be handled, and the Wizard's Lab is filled with do-it-yourself experiments dealing with such things pendulums, air cars, and magnets.

Just outside the back door of the museum is a mock-up of the nose of the space shuttle Challenger. The cockpit is open for tours some weekends during the summer.

Directions: East on Hearst Avenue, right on Gayley, and follow the signs.
Phone: (510) 642-5132.
Hours: Monday - Friday, 10 a.m. to 4:30 p.m.; Saturday and Sunday, 10 a.m. to 5 p.m. The Planetarium, the Biology Lab, and the Wizard's Lab are open daily during the summer; weekends, holidays the rest of the year.
Admission: Adults $5.00; Students, Seniors $4.00; Children (3–6) $2.00.
Parking: Free.
Age Range: All ages.
Wheelchair Access: Yes, except for the planetarium and space shuttle.

Lindsay Museum

1901 First Avenue (at Buena Vista), Walnut Creek.

Having recently moved into an attractive new building, the Lindsay Museum is home to wild animals that have been injured or orphaned and can no longer be released back to the wild. Animals such as birds with damaged wings, blind snakes, and squirrels and others that have been raised as house pets, end up here. The museum's objective is to teach children (and adults) about mankind's impact on the natural world and how to be more sensitive to the needs of wildlife.

The light and airy new facility is designed to offer maximum opportunities to get close to the animals. Especially effective are the open-air exhibits containing the birds. Securely tethered, they sit on perches that are high enough to be out of reach yet near enough so you can see up close a variety of hawks, falcons, and other birds of prey. No cages or protective glass bar the view.

The birds sit atop plexiglas cages that hold such things as a bobcat, a fox, a squirrel, and other native California species. Across the hall, a terrarium and aquarium hold turtles, salamanders, minnows, and various fish. An information board points up the dangers that water pollution poses for these creatures.

Not all the animals are alive. An eye-catching scene at the end of the hall is a full-size replica of Balancing Rock, an actual outcropping on nearby Mt. Diablo. Positioned on and around the rock are mounted examples of local fauna — a black-tailed deer, a coyote, and a peregrine falcon, to name a few. Perched on top of the rock is a young mountain lion.

Phone: (510) 935-1978.
Hours: Wednesday - Sunday, 1 p.m. to 5 p.m.
Admission: Adults (18–64) $3.00; Seniors (65+) $2.00;
Children (3–17) $2.00.
Parking: Free lot.
Age Range: All ages.
Wheelchair Access: Yes.

Palo Alto Junior Museum and Zoo

1451 Middlefield Road (near Embarcadero), Palo Alto.

This museum features exhibitions that change yearly. In previous years the exhibits have focused on such things as trains, airplanes, and underwater sea life. Recently the subject was trees and forests. It highlighted the different kinds of forests, the varying sylvan climates, and the animals to be found in each.

Since the target age range is young children, experiments tend to emphasize hands-on activities. In the trees and forests exhibit, for example, there were buttons to push so that kids could learn about such things as photosynthesis and how trees grow. They could also push a button to activate a miniature train that circled through a lumber camp.

Although most of the space in this one-room museum is given over to temporary exhibitions, there are a few permanent displays. The most notable is the one on carniverous plants. Under glass are living specimens of some of the more renowned examples — pitcher plants, sundews, bladderworts, and the ever popular Venus fly trap. The descriptive panels describing them are particularly informative in explaining how these plants operate to attract and digest their prey, and why they evolved as carnivores.

Adjoining the museum is a small zoo. In large cages or behind glass are various native California and foreign animals. There are raccoons, ravens, and a great horned owl, as well as an iguana, a boa constrictor, and several other kinds of snakes. In the center of the zoo is a pond filled with ducks, geese, and turtles. This is not a petting zoo, however, so children should keep a distance from the fence and the sometimes noisy geese who come to the rail.

Phone: (415) 329-2111.
Hours: Tuesday - Saturday, 10 a.m. to 5 p.m.; Sunday, 1 p.m. to 4 p.m.
Admission: Free.
Parking: There is a free lot in front of the museum.
Age Range: 2 to 10 years.
Wheelchair Access: Yes.

Randall Museum

199 Museum Way (at the south end of Masonic Avenue), San Francisco.

This small museum with a friendly staff is designed to inspire children to develop lifelong interests in nature, art, and science.

Animals are always a popular attraction at children's museums; the main draw here is the petting corral. Children can enter an enclosed pen stocked with ducks, chickens, and a lop-eared rabbit, and pet these tame creatures.

Surrounding the petting corral are other live animals, most of them native to California. You can get up close to cages or glass enclosures and see raccoons, turtles, toads, and various kinds of birds. Among the latter are several kinds of hawks, which are securely tethered to open-air perches above the cages. Also note the beautiful pair of multi-striped San Francisco garter snakes, a rare and endangered species.

The museum's wings house various workshops, which sponsor classes in activities such as ceramics, woodworking, lapidary and jewelry, and art. Most of the classes last six sessions, but each Saturday there are one-day classes on various topics. On the second and fourth Saturdays each month you can watch members of the Golden Gate Model Railroad Club operate their elaborate model train in the basement.

Either before or after visiting the museum you can enjoy a nice view of San Francisco by climbing to the summit of Corona Heights Park, behind the museum. For the less energetic, good views are to be had from the museum's parking lot.

Phone: (415) 554-9600.
Hours: Tuesday - Saturday, 10 a.m. to 5 p.m. (The animal room closes from 1 to 2 p.m.)
Admission: Free. Saturday classes charge a nominal entry fee.
Parking: Free lot.
Age Range: All Ages.
Wheelchair Access: Yes.

San Francisco Neighborhoods

The annual Union Street fair always draws festive throngs.

The Castro

Bounded by Dolores, Douglass, 16th, and 22nd streets.

The Castro is the heart of San Francisco's gay community. Although gays and lesbians live all over The City, here they predominate; 85% of the Castro's population is estimated to be gay.

The Castro's heavy gay coloration is a relatively recent phenomenon. Until the early 1970s the district was inhabited mainly by middle-class San Franciscans of Italian and Irish descent. But between 1972 and 1974 the neighborhood was transformed as gays moved in, establishing their own community in the process. What was once known as the Most Holy Redeemer Parish became San Francisco's answer to New York's Fire Island.

Experiencing a simultaneous political and sexual liberation, neighborhood residents engaged in all sorts of uninhibited behavior. The anything-goes mentality continued until the early 1980s, when AIDS made its deadly debut. The Names Project, at 2362A Market Street, and the famous AIDS quilt that continues to grow from it, documents this ongoing tragedy.

The neighborhood's crossroads is the intersection of Castro and 18th streets. There are gay bars, a bookstore specializing in books on gay topics, and other businesses serving the community.

Whether you are straight or gay, the Castro is worth a visit, if for no other reason than to people-watch. Also evident, even to the casual observer, is the real sense of community that prevails here. The neighborhood is one of the cleanest in the city and also one of the safest after dark.

Parking: There is metered street parking in the commercial area; nearby residential streets have a two-hour limit.
Wheelchair Access: Good in the immediate vicinity of Castro and 18th streets.

Chinatown

The district's core can be found between Broadway, Kearny, California, and Stockton streets. The Chinatown gate at Bush and California marks the official entrance to Chinatown.

Chinatown teems with life. During the day you will find its sidewalks crowded with Asians doing their food shopping; in the evening, locals and tourists predominate, shopping or dining in the numerous restaurants found here.

Grant Avenue, from Bush to Broadway, is the district's throbbing main artery. This is where you will find the majority of retail stores. The emphasis is on jewelry and low-end knicknacks and souvenirs, but high priced jade and ivory can also be found here. A little-noticed bronze plaque at 823 Grant Avenue marks the approximate location of the San Francisco's first dwelling.

For a look at Chinatown as its residents know it walk along the west side of Stockton Street between Jackson and Broadway. This is where many of the food markets are located. On Saturdays the sidewalks here can be so crowded that it's hard to move. Customers elbow their way through the crowds to select fresh fruit and vegetables directly from boxes; ducks suspended from hooks, dripping juices into steel pans; and live animals ranging from turtles and bull frogs to chickens and other birds.

You can experience more of the "authentic" Chinatown by visiting a Chinese temple. There are several open to the public, but the Tin How Temple located at 125 Waverly is the oldest. Located on the top floor of a four-story building (no elevator), you will find a small room densely packed with an altar and ritual objects — statues of deities, urns burning incense, and a multitude of small golden lanterns suspended from the ceiling.

Hours: The Tin How Temple is open daily 10:00 a.m. to 5 p.m.
Parking: Street parking in this congested area is difficult. Try either the garage under Portsmouth Square or the Stockton-Sutter garage.
Wheelchair Access: Generally good along Broadway, and the north-south streets — Kearny, Grant, and Stockton; less so on the east-west streets.

Civic Center

Bounded by Golden Gate Avenue and Hyde, Hayes, and Franklin streets.

San Francisco's Civic Center is thought by many architects and historians to be the premier example in the United States of a Classical or Beaux-Arts style municipal government complex. Because of this, it was entered on the National Register of Historic Places by the federal government in 1987.

The centerpiece is the Renaissance Revival City Hall, constructed in 1915. Beautifully proportioned both inside and out, it projects an aura of imperial grandeur. In the wake of the 1906 earthquake, and a concurrent graft trial involving the mayor, nothing did more to restore San Franciscans pride in their city than the erection of this edifice.

Around the plaza, which fronts City Hall on Polk Street, are other Beaux-Arts style buildings — the Exposition Auditorium, erected in 1915 (now called the Bill Graham Civic Auditorium), the State of California Building (1925), and the Main Library (1917). All of them are undergoing change. Both the Auditorium and the State Building are currently closed for seismic upgrading. And the Main Library will move in 1995 to a new building being erected just across Fulton Street from the present structure.

Behind City Hall, across Van Ness Avenue, are the War Memorial Opera House and the Veterans Auditorium Building. Constructed during 1931–32, they retain the Beaux-Arts style of the rest of the complex. A new addition to the Center, located across Grove Street from the Opera House, is Davies Symphony Hall. This modern, curvilinear building with floor-to-ceiling windows (at night it becomes a temple of light), opened in 1981. As the name implies, it is home to the San Francisco Symphony.

Parking: There is a garage under the Civic Center plaza (entrance on McAllister Street), and metered spaces also abound in the area. **Wheelchair Access:** The area is on level ground; all the buildings are accessible.

The Embarcadero

The Embarcadero is the esplanade that fronts the bay along the north-east corner of the city.

The tragedy of the 1989 earthquake proved a blessing in one respect — the view-destroying Embarcadero Freeway was damaged badly enough that it had to be taken down. Its removal has opened vistas not seen since the 1950s.

The Ferry Building (see p. 52) stands at the center of the Embarcadero. Spanish Mission-style piers flank it on each side and extend to Fisherman's Wharf (p. 121) and PIER 39 (p. 131) at the north end and to China Basin at the south end. The piers are little used today, since much of the Bay Area shipping has moved to Oakland's deep water port.

With the freeway gone and with many of the piers underutilized, the Embarcadero will be seeing changes coming in the next few years and into the 21st century. Construction is already underway to extend Muni streetcars along the Embarcadero and turn it into a palm-tree-lined boulevard.

The best place to find out more about the past and future of this strip of land is at the Rincon Center on Mission Street between Steuart and Spear streets. This former main post office has been converted to an office tower, but the old lobby has been retained along with some interesting WPA-era murals.

Glass cases along the north wall hold artifacts found during excavation, which recall a time when this area was a neighborhood of coal and lumber yards, ship chandlers, and sailors' boardinghouses. Farther back in the lobby, past the dramatic rain column that cascades from the ceiling, is a model and drawings of proposed changes to come along the Embarcadero.

Parking: There are short term parking meters along much of the Embarcadero. Parking garages in the nearby downtown area tend to be expensive.
Wheelchair Access: This is one of the few neighborhoods in The City that is completely flat.

Financial District

Bounded by Market, Kearny, Washington, and Drumm streets.

The Financial District is home to San Francisco's largest employers and businesses. Its skyscrapers house the offices of major banks, insurance companies, and law firms. International companies, Chevron/Standard Oil and Bechtel Engineering among them, have their headquarters here.

Montgomery Street, sometimes called "Wall Street West," has long been a prestigious address. The Mills Building (1891) at 220 Montgomery was one of the few office buildings to survive 1906. This Romanesque Revival structure was gutted, but its exterior walls remained standing. The lobby has a beautiful carved balustrade of veined marble leading to the second floor.

Across the street, occupying the whole block, is the handsome Russ Building (1927). Notice how it resembles a cathedral. This motif is carried on both in the area framing the front door with its niches for statues of saints, and inside with its Gothic groin vaulted ceilings in the lobby.

A block and a half away is an architectural gem, the Hallidie Building (1917) at 130–150 Sutter Street. Its glass facade, the first of its kind, makes this a special building. Across the street is the Crocker Galleria, a light and airy shopping mall covered by a glass dome. The top floor has a wide variety of restaurants.

The best panoramic views in the city are to be had just blocks from here. The Carnelian Room bar and restaurant on the 52nd floor of the Bank of America Building, California and Montgomery streets, is open to the public weekdays from 3 p.m. The view is spectacular. The Transamerica Pyramid, Montgomery and Clay streets, has a viewing area on its 27th floor: a good view also but only to the north.

Parking: Garages here are quite expensive during the day. Try the city-owned Stockton-Sutter garage; the rates are reasonable.
Wheelchair Access: The area is mostly flat; the buildings are accessible.

Haight-Ashbury

Located south of the Golden Gate Park Panhandle. The heart of the district is Haight Street between Stanyan and Central.

The name Haight-Ashbury today is virtually synonymous with the youth rebellion of the 1960s. Hippies and the 1967 "Summer of Love" were chronicled the world over.

Nothing in its 19th-century beginnings foreshadowed what the neighborhood was to become. Starting in the 1880s "The Haight," as it is popularly known, developed into a suburban resort/recreation area. Many of San Francisco's wealthier families built second homes here. Nearby Golden Gate Park was a popular weekend destination.

The Great Depression of the 1930s led to a decades-long decline of the once upper-crust area. After World War II black former shipyard workers and others looking for cheap rents moved in.

The Summer of Love proved a turning point: it changed the name Haight-Ashbury from just another San Francisco suburb to something much more. Today only a few remnants of that era remain. The most notable is the Haight-Ashbury Free Clinic at Haight and Stanyan streets, which has been operating at that same location since it opened in June 1967.

Although the bell bottoms and love beads of a generation ago have disappeared, the Haight today still retains much the same flavor it did then. The best way to experience it is to walk the main commercial part of Haight Street, or, better yet, grab a window table at one of the bars, coffeehouses, or ice cream shops and watch the parade go by. You will see some of the strangest clothing and hair styles this side of New York's Greenwich Village.

Parking: Metered spaces on Haight Street or two-hour limit on nearby side streets. Oak Street along the Panhandle usually has spaces.
Wheelchair Access: Good along Haight and adjacent cross streets.

Jackson Square

Located in the northeast corner of San Francisco, it is bounded by
Washington, Columbus, Pacific, and Sansome streets.

Designated as San Francisco's first historic district, Jackson
Square contains The City's oldest commercial buildings — dating
from the 1850s and 1860s. This was also the location of the notorious Barbary Coast, home to raucous saloons, dancehalls, and
bawdy-houses during the 19th and early 20th centuries.

This quarter originally was the commercial and financial center of the city, and as such its mainly two- and three-story brick
buildings housed shops, banks, offices, and warehouses. Today,
having weathered nearly a century and a half of change (including the 1906 earthquake and fire), these historic structures are
largely inhabited by antique dealers, art galleries, and law firms.

The 400 block of Jackson Street (between Montgomery and
Sansome) is the heart of the district. On the northeast corner of
Montgomery and Jackson is a two-story building known as "Sherman's Bank," because in the 1850s future Civil War general William Tecumseh Sherman managed a bank at this location. The
rather plain two-story brick building next door at 472 Jackson,
with its original cast-iron shutters on the second floor, is a classic
example of the type of Yankee commercial architecture that went
up in many northern California towns in the 1850s. It was constructed sometime between 1850 and 1852.

The most elegant building on the block is the 1866 Italianate
Hotaling warehouse across the street at 451 Jackson. Hotaling was
a liquor merchant. Legend has it that this building and others in
the area were saved in 1906 because Hotaling promised firefight-
ers free bottles of whiskey if they would save his business.

Parking: The streets are lined with parking meters, but the closest and
least expensive garage is at Portsmouth Square a few blocks southwest at
Clay and Kearny streets.
Wheelchair Access: The area is fairly flat, although Montgomery Street
north of Jackson is a bit of a grade.

Japantown

The heart of the district is bordered by Geary Boulevard and Fillmore, Sutter, and Laguna streets.

If you like sushi, tempura, and other Japanese dishes, you'll love Japantown; it's chock-a-block with sushi bars and restaurants. There is, however, more here than places to eat. Japantown has a variety of other shops. You can buy antique Japanese chests, tea pots and cups, fine art, or even ikebana — traditional Japanese flower arrangements.

Although the name Japantown implies an ethnic enclave like Chinatown, few Japanese-Americans actually live here. The name is a legacy of World War II hysteria that led to this ethnic group being removed from their neighborhood as alleged subversives. They were unjustly interred in camps in several western states. This uprooting was further exacerbated by redevelopment in the 1950s and 1960s, which, under the guise of "urban renewal," led to the wholesale demolition of Victorian houses once inhabited by Japanese-Americans.

What replaced it now forms the heart of today's Japantown — Japan Center, extending from the Miyako Hotel at Laguna Street to the Kabuki movie theatre at Fillmore Street, and the Buchanan Street Mall, a short one-block-long pedestrian mall between Post and Sutter streets. Japan Center is mainly an enclosed mall full of restaurants and shops. The covered bridge over Webster Street is the only one in San Francisco that houses commercial businesses.

Great times to visit Japantown are in April when the cherry blossom festival is held, or in August, when on two successive weekends the Nihonmachi street fair takes place. Crowds throng the area to eat carryout food from sidewalk vendors and to see traditional Japanese entertainment.

Parking: There is a city-owned garage under the Japantown Center (entrance on Geary) and street parking abounds nearby.
Wheelchair Access: The Japan Center mall is accessible from Post Street at Buchanan.

The Marina

Bounded by Laguna, Lombard, and Lyon streets, and on the north by San Francisco Bay.

The Marina, one of The City's finer residential areas, occupies the stretch of the north waterfront that hosted San Francisco's world's fair of 1915, the Panama Pacific International Exposition. The only building not demolished when the fair closed was the Palace of Fine Arts (see p. 68). In the 1920s developers laid out streets on the former fairgrounds and erected the mostly stucco and brick apartment buildings standing there today.

When the Loma Prieta earthquake struck in 1989, the Marina was hard hit — the area is mainly built on landfill. Many buildings suffered damage; a few collapsed outright. The recovery here was swift, however. About the only reminder of the quake visible today is a clutch of shiny new apartment buildings that replaced a number of destroyed units.

The neighborhood's main commercial boulevard is Chestnut Street, from Fillmore to Divisadero. It is notable for its great number of eating and drinking establishments. There are coffee bars, delis, markets, and a wide range of restaurants.

The Marina's most delightful feature is the Marina Green, a large stretch of green lawn bordering the shoreline. It is a magnet, particularly on weekends, for joggers, kiteflyers, and picnickers. A separate patch of green at the west end, next to the Presidio, attracts sunbathers and volleyball enthusiasts.

From the west end of the green, if you stroll over to the water and east past the St. Francis and Golden Gate Yacht clubs, you will be treated to unimpeded views of the Golden Gate Bridge, Alcatraz, and the bay. Look south and you'll see a slice of the city from the Palace of Fine Arts to the tallest spires of the Financial district.

Parking: Free parking can usually be found on Fillmore between Chestnut and Marina Drive. The Marina Green has plenty of free parking. **Wheelchair Access:** Excellent; the Marina is on level ground.

The Mission District

Bounded by Potrero Avenue and Army, Church, and 14th streets.

The immigrant experience is an almost mythic part of America's heritage. To see first hand the latest wave, visit the Mission District where refugees from strife-torn Central America are settling in. Once home to a mix of largely German, Irish, and Italian working-class families, the Mission is now more than 50% Latino.

Mission Street, from 16th to 24th streets, is the main drag. But to really get the flavor of this neighborhood, stroll down 24th Street between Mission and Hampshire (but not after dark). This is the Mission's consumer and cultural heart — it's lined with restaurants, bars, bakeries, produce markets, and shops selling all manner of "productos de Latino America."

Also along this stretch of 24th Street are some fine examples of the colorful outdoor art that has enlivened the Mission in recent years: murals. One of the best wraps around the southwest corner of 24th and Florida streets. Entitled "500 Years of Resistance," this vivid mural of bright colors and expressive faces, like many of the ones here, speaks to themes of social injustice and oppression.

Nearby is Balmy Alley, a one-block street considered to be the lodestar of the mural movement; every fence and garage door is decorated. Some of the murals carry political messages, others seem strictly for decorative effect. (City Guides, a local group, gives free walking tours of the Mission murals. Call (415) 557-4266 for information.)

In the Mission district's northwest corner is the landmark for which the neighborhood is named: Mission Dolores (p. 61). Two blocks south is Dolores Park. There is a fine view of the high rises of downtown San Francisco from the park's southwest corner.

Parking: There is street parking, and a garage with moderate rates at 21st and Bartlett (enter on 21st). BART has stations at 16th and 24th streets.
Wheelchair Access: Streets are level, except as you approach Dolores Heights in the southwest corner of the district.

Nob Hill

Bounded by Pacific Avenue and Powell, Bush, and Hyde streets.

Of all of San Francisco's 40-some-odd hills, Nob Hill is the most famous. In the late 19th century it was, as author Robert Louis Stevenson called it, "the Hill of Palaces," because on its crest stood the extravagant mansions of the city's moneyed elite.

Nob Hill initially was little more than a sparsely settled promontory. It was the invention of the cable car in 1873 that made the city's hills accessible and led to their rapid development. Railroad baron Leland Stanford, his partners, and, later, Comstock millionaire James Flood, built lavish homes next door to each other.

The 1906 fire swept them all away. Only the Flood mansion (on California Street between Mason and Pleasant), which was gutted, was rebuilt, since its exterior walls were of stone rather than wood as were the others. The Flood mansion today houses the Pacific Union Club, a private mens club.

Huntington Park, next door, is a small, green oasis that provides relief from the surrounding high-rise luxury hotels and apartments that have gone up since 1906. The delightful fountain in the center of the park is a copy of a 16th-century Roman one.

Across Taylor Street from the park is the Gothic-style Grace Cathedral, one of the most impressive churches in San Francisco. Notice especially the gleaming bronze door in the portal of the east facade, with its biblical scenes and realistic modeled heads. The remaining granite wall surrounding the block provides a reminder of the 1906 fire: its black patina and missing flecks and chips were caused by the great heat from that blaze.

There are panoramic views from the rooftop cocktail lounges at the Fairmount and Mark Hopkins hotels.

Parking: Street parking is always tight, and garages expensive, so why not take the cable car? All three lines cross at Powell and California. **Wheelchair Access:** Only the block surrounded by Mason, California, Taylor, and Sacramento streets is readily accessible.

Noe Valley

Bounded by Church, Hoffman, 22nd, and 26th streets.

Named for Jose Noe, the last Mexican alcalde (mayor) of San Francisco, who owned a ranch spread over the area, Noe Valley is one of The City's most diverse neighborhoods. Here'll you'll find people of every stripe: young and old; white, black, Hispanic, and Asian; families and singles; straights and gays.

Although some isolated Victorian houses were built here as early as the 1870s, it wasn't until 1888, when a cable car line was extended along Castro to 24th Street, that the area really started to develop. The population increased further after 1906, when refugees migrated here after the earthquake.

The communal/social heart of the district is 24th Street between Church and Diamond streets. It is a pleasant place for a stroll, for besides the usual community small businesses — a supermarket, a real estate office, pharmacy, bakery, and others — it is lined with cafes, coffeehouses, and bars. A number of attractive restaurants have opened in recent years.

The nearby residential streets, in this usually sunny enclave, are a great place for a walk, especially if you appreciate Victorian architecture. There are many examples of the Stick and Queen Anne styles. Virtually all are in a fine state of preservation.

Despite the fact that most of the neighborhood lies in a valley, it rises swiftly in elevation to the south. On Sanchez Street at both 21st and at Hill Street there are superb views of the city and the bay. Looking south from Sanchez you will be treated to a great cityscape view. This is a view of the real San Francisco — this is where its people live.

Parking: There is metered street parking in the 24th Street commercial area; most nearby residential streets have a two-hour limit.
Wheelchair Access: Good along 24th Street; less so elsewhere.

North Beach

Bounded by Montgomery, Pacific, Mason, and Greenwich streets.

Colorful North Beach, one of San Francisco's oldest neighbor-hoods, lies in a valley nestled between Russian and Telegraph hills. At one time there was an actual beach on the north water-front — hence the name — but increasing industrialization had filled in its cove and covered the beach by the late 1870s.

Because of a concentration of Italian fishermen and shopkeep-ers in the district from the 1890s to the 1950s, it became known as San Francisco's "Little Italy." It's a moniker that still fits today, especially because of the many Italian restaurants here, but Chi-natown has spilled north of Broadway, encroaching on it.

In the mid-1950s "beatniks" made North Beach their home, leading to a reputation that North Beach still retains today, that of a bohemian enclave. The Beat movement, with its poetry readings and love of jazz, lasted only a few years, but it left a couple of landmarks that still thrive today — City Lights Books and Vesuvio Cafe. Both were hangouts for Jack Keroauc, Allen Ginsberg, and others.

In the 1960s North Beach further increased its notoriety when topless, and then bottomless, nightclubs opened along Broadway near Columbus. Changing times have led to the covering of some of the flesh; the number of clubs has also dwindled.

Nevertheless, North Beach offers The City's greatest concen-tration of nightlife and entertainment. The area comes alive at night and on weekends when crowds throng the streets. Colum-bus Avenue, Broadway, and Grant Avenue north of Broadway are where the action is. The latter street especially, with its funky bars and shops, retains the area's bohemian flavor.

Parking: It's very tough to find street parking here. The closest garage with reasonable rates is under Portsmouth Square in Chinatown. **Wheelchair Access:** Most of the district is navigable.

Pacific Heights

Located in the city's Western Addition, the boundaries are generally defined as Van Ness Avenue, California Street, Presidio Avenue, and Green Street.

Pacific Heights is San Francisco's choicest residential neighborhood. This is where many of the City's wealthiest inhabitants live.

If you appreciate fine architecture and great views, Pacific Heights is a feast for the eyes. Grand houses and mansions are found throughout the district, but the most stunning examples can be seen on outer Broadway between Divisadero and Lyon streets. The houses on the north side of the street hug a steep ridge overlooking the northern portion of the city, the bay, and the hills beyond. You can share some of the superb views these houses enjoy from the sidewalks on Broadway at the intersection of Broderick and also at Lyon Street.

A few blocks farther east — at 2222 Broadway — is the former James Leary Flood mansion, erected in 1913. Clad in pale pink Tennessee marble, this Italian Renaissance Revival structure has been called "the stateliest house ever erected in San Francisco." If the gate to the children's playground next door is open, walk back to the courtyard for a glimpse of the beautifully detailed bay window framing what was the drawing room.

Two other areas where fine homes are clustered are near Pacific Heights's two major parks — Alta Plaza and Lafayette Square. Slicing through a valley between them is Fillmore Street, the area's main retail district. It is lined with fine shops, restaurants, bars, and coffee houses. It's a great place to relax and take a load off your feet after exploring the neighborhood on foot.

Parking: Street parking is relatively easy to find in this part of town.
Wheelchair Access: Parts of the district are quite hilly but the sections of Broadway mentioned above are on level ground.

Russian Hill

Bounded by Pacific Avenue and Taylor, Francisco, and Polk streets.

Russian Hill, once a Bohemian enclave that attracted writers and artists to its slopes, is now one of the more prestigious addresses in San Francisco. It occupies a zigzag ridge near downtown and offers great views of the financial district, North Beach, and the bay.

The hill's summit is located on Vallejo Street between Taylor and Jones. The hill derived its name from this plot because in the mid-19th century this area was a graveyard for Russian sailors. The semicircular balustrade at the street's deadend affords a fine view of North Beach.

A block to the south, at the Broadway bulkhead (walk through Florence Alley and go down the steps), is a superb view of the high rises of the financial district. It is especially dramatic at night when the buildings are lit up.

Macondray Lane, two and a half blocks north of Broadway via Jones Street, offers a glimpse of the "hidden" Russian Hill. This charming pedestrian lane, with its brick sidewalk and profusion of sheltering vegetation, gives an idea of Russian Hill's attraction as a place to live.

Some blocks away, the Hill's north slope also offers fine views, primarily of the north waterfront and the bay. It also is the site of George Sterling Park, named for the San Francisco poet. Just across Hyde Street from the park is the famous Lombard "crookedest" Street (see p. 124). Not far away is the San Francisco Art Institute. It's a fine place to end a tour of Russian Hill; you can enjoy fine views and a meal in the roof deck cafeteria.

Parking: There are no parking garages near Russian Hill, and street parking can be tough. Cable car or bus are good ways to access the hill. **Wheelchair Access:** Only a few streets in the areas mentioned above are level — Broadway above the bulkhead, Jones north to Green Street, and Hyde Street between Greenwich and Lombard.

South of Market

Bounded by Market Street, the Embarcadero, China Basin, and Division and 13th streets. South Park is enclosed in the block bordered by Bryant, Brannan, 2nd, and 3rd streets.

During the 19th century, South of Market, with the exception of choice Rincon Hill, was a mostly working-class neighborhood whose streets were lined with Victorian row houses. The 1906 fire reduced all of it to ashes. Warehouses and small manufacturing arose in its place, and the area became heavily industrial.

South of Market today is a neighborhood in transition. Now frequently referred to as SoMa, a borrowing from to New York's SoHo, it has lately taken on a bohemian reputation, attracting artists, musicians, and small businesses of various kinds. Restaurants, bars, and nightclubs have sprung up, and more recently, old warehouses have been converted to live-and-work lofts, further increasing the area's appeal. This has led to some odd juxtapositions: a trendy new restaurant stands next to a tire shop.

In contrast to other city neighborhoods, most of which have a "center" or main commercial strip, SoMa has no such area; restaurants, bars, and businesses are dotted all over.

Because of its recent industrial history, SoMa has only a few patches of green. The most notable is South Park, an oval lawn ringed with trees. After spending much of the 20th-century in rather sad shape, South Park has undergone a renaissance in just the past few years. Several attractive cafes and restaurants have opened, drawing crowds and breathing new life into the area.

Across 2nd Street from South Park is a charming champagne bar, Cava 555. A small jazz combo plays from an elevated perch above the bar. A few doors up is the Capp Street Project, an avant-garde art gallery.

Parking: Street parking is relatively easy here. For daytime parking, meters are prevalent from about Mission Street up to Folsom; one and two hour zones start beyond there.
Wheelchair Access: The area is almost entirely level.

Telegraph Hill

Located in the northeast corner of San Francisco. Access by auto or bus is via Lombard Street.

Telegraph Hill is one of San Francisco's most charming neighborhoods. Houses on its eastern slope survived the 1906 fire, preserving some of The City's oldest dwellings. Legend has it that the buildings were saved by residents who doused their homes with wine as the flames approached.

The hill derives its name from a semaphore station that stood atop the summit in the early 1850s. It was used to signal the arrival of ships in the bay. In the 1930s the hill's signature structure, Coit Tower (see p. 48), rose from the site of the long-gone semaphore station.

To see some of the dwellings that give Telegraph Hill its unique character, walk down the Filbert Street steps. From the bend in the curve leading to Coit Tower, descend these steps down the hill's eastern slope. Continue past Montgomery Street and you will quickly find yourself on a wooden walkway amid an eden-like garden that is lovingly tended by the area residents. The Carpenter Gothic-style Victorian cottages here date from the 1860s and 1870s.

Just a half block to the south at 31 Alta Street is one of the oldest houses in San Francisco. This three-story house with two balconies was built in 1852.

On the way back up the Filbert steps to get to Alta Street take a look at a 20th-century building of note — 1360 Montgomery Street. This stylish Art Deco apartment house (now condos) was constructed in 1936. It served as a backdrop in the 1947 movie *Dark Passage*, starring Humphrey Bogart and Lauren Bacall.

Parking: Street parking here is some of the hardest to find in The City. Your best bet is to take a cab or the Muni — either the Coit Tower or Union Street bus.
Wheelchair Access: With nothing but steep grades and stairs, this is tough territory for the disabled.

Union Square

Bounded by Geary, Powell, Post, and Stockton streets.

The Union Square area is San Francisco's premier shopping district. The emphasis is on fashionable clothing and luxury goods. Surrounding this heart-of-downtown park are such retailers as Macys, I. Magnin, Neiman Marcus, Tiffany, and Saks.

Union Square is San Francisco's second oldest park, having been deeded for public use in January 1850. It received its name in 1860 when pro-Union rallies were held here prior to the Civil War.

The tall column in the center of the plaza was erected in 1901 to commemorate Admiral Dewey's victory over the Spanish fleet at Manila Bay during the Spanish-American war. The parking garage underneath was added in 1942. The park itself, although not unsafe, unfortunately attracts a good number of the down-on-their-luck, not to mention pigeons.

Across Powell Street from the Square stands one of San Francisco's truly grand hotels, the St. Francis. Erected in 1904 (and gutted in the 1906 fire), the restored lobby, with its marble floor, serpentine Corinthian columns, and coffered terracotta ceiling recalls a more opulent era. The elegant Compass Rose bar, just off the lobby, serves lunch and afternoon tea.

On the other side of the Square begins a two-block alley, Maiden Lane. Prior to 1906 this thoroughfare was lined with the city's most notorious bawdy houses. Today, closed to vehicular traffic, it houses fine shops and a Parisian-style cafe with outdoor tables. A notable piece of architecture is the Circle Gallery building at number 140, designed by Frank Lloyd Wright. Its interior circular ramp resembles Wright's later design for the Guggenheim Museum in New York.

Parking: Try the garage under the Square, but public transit is best.
Wheelchair Access: Check with individual shops, but the major ones and the St. Francis Hotel are accessible.

Union Street / Cow Hollow

Cow Hollow is bounded by Van Ness Avenue and Green, Lyon, and Lombard streets. Union Street runs parallel to Green Street, one block north of it.

Union Street, home to stylish shops and restaurants, is part of an area known as Cow Hollow, which is sandwiched between the northern slope of Pacific Heights and the Marina district. In the 19th century it was home to a number of dairy farms — hence the name Cow Hollow.

Union Street's transformation from a typical Victorian/Edwardian-era residential district to its current incarnation as an upscale shopping mecca, started in the 1950s. Parking meters were installed and Victorian houses lining the street were converted into storefronts. Today, Union Street from Gough to Fillmore is home to a broad array of specialty shops, art galleries, boutiques, and restaurants. Union Street and Fillmore Street from Union to Lombard are also home to numerous popular singles bars.

Because the 1906 earthquake and fire spared Cow Hollow, a number of notable buildings still stand. One of the more visible, yet invisible since it has been converted entirely into retail space, is the house at 2040 Union Street. This 1873 Victorian was the home of dairy rancher James Cudworth. One block down, at 1980 Union, are twin houses, also housing shops, that Cudworth built as wedding presents for his two daughters.

Also worth a look are the Octagon House (see p. 65); the Vedanta Temple (1905) with its odd onion-dome roof, at Filbert and Webster, home to a religious order; the Casebolt House (1866) at 2727 Pierce Street, a grand Italianate manor; and the Sherman House (1876) at 2160 Green Street. The latter now operates as an exclusive hotel and restaurant.

Parking: Parking is tough to find in this neighborhood, especially on weekends. Nearby residential streets have a daytime two-hour limit. **Wheelchair Access:** Good from Union Street north.

Yerba Buena Gardens

The city block bounded by Mission, Howard, Third, and Fourth streets.

Yerba Buena Gardens is San Francisco's newest "neighborhood." This art and entertainment complex, almost 30 years in planning and development, opened in October 1993 in an area that was formerly San Francisco's skid row.

The two major buildings anchoring the complex — both facing Third Street — are the Center for the Arts Galleries and Forum, a complex housing three art galleries and a small film/video theater, and the 755-seat Center for the Arts Theater.

Behind these two buildings is the Esplanade, an oval 5½-acre grassy meadow. The plaza surrounding the oval holds sculpture and other works of art. Just south of the oval is a 50-foot-long and 20-foot-high silvery waterfall dedicated to Martin Luther King Jr. Adorning the granite wall behind the waterfall are quotes from Dr. King's speeches and writings.

On the terrace level above the waterfall are a promenade and two light and airy cafes. Both cafes have outdoor patios, which, when the weather is nice, make them delightful places to sit, relax, and enjoy the view of the Esplanade and the tall buildings of downtown San Francisco in the background.

More attractions are coming in the next few years, most notably the San Francisco Museum of Modern Art. It moves to its new building on Third Street between Mission and Howard in 1995. With the addition of several other museums, and construction of movie theaters west of the Esplanade along Fourth Street in 1996, Yerba Buena Gardens promises to be one of the premier performing and visual arts centers in the country.

Phone: Galleries and Forum: (415) 978-2700; Theater: (415) 978-2787.
Hours: Galleries and Forum is open Tuesday - Sunday, 11 a.m. to 6 p.m.
Admission: Galleries and Forum: Adults $3.00; Seniors $1.00; Children (under 16) $1.00. Free the first Thursday each month from 6 p.m. to 9 p.m.
Parking: Fifth and Mission garage is cheapest and closest.
Wheelchair Access: Yes.

Beyond the Bay

Nevada City's old firehouse—heart of the Gold Country.

Gold Rush Country

The heart of the Gold Country is Highway 49, located in the Sierra Nevada foothills roughly 150 miles east of San Francisco.

The California gold rush is one of the famous events in American history. It started in January 1848 when James Marshall, the foreman of a group of men constructing a sawmill, found gold nuggets in the mill's tailrace. The word of the discovery quickly spread around the world, and by 1849 a mass migration to California was under way.

A good introduction to the area's history is provided by five state historic parks along historic Highway 49.

Columbia State Historic Park, (209) 532-4301. Located two miles north of Sonora, Columbia was established as a park by the state legislature in 1945 because it represented an opportunity to preserve what was still a fairly intact gold-rush town. The main streets are closed to vehicles, and thus you can wander at leisure and peer into the buildings, which have mostly been restored to their 1850s' appearance. Main Street has a Wells Fargo building, a stage coach office, and a blacksmith shop, among others. Also of interest are some of the shops on the side streets — a drugstore; a dentist's office; and a Chinese herb shop.

Indian Grinding Rock State Historic Park, (209) 296-7488. Located off Highway 88 eight miles east of Jackson, the only non-gold-rush park of the five, Indian Grinding Rock documents the lives of the Miwok Indians who inhabited this area before the gold seekers arrived. Set in a meadow surrounded by valley oaks is a remarkable object — a large slab of rock covered with over a thousand mortar holes. The Miwoks created them in the process of grinding acorns and seeds into meal. There is a visitor center and museum on the bluff overlooking the site.

Marshall Gold Discovery State Historic Park, (916) 622-3470. In the little town of Coloma is where Marshall found the first nuggets — the birthplace of the gold rush. Start at the visitor center and museum for a general orientation. Across Highway 49, next to the picturesque American River, is a replica of the famous sawmill. A little farther downstream you can see the remains of the tailrace and the spot where Marshall first spied the precious metal.

Empire Mine State Historic Park, (916) 273-8522. Located less than two miles outside the town of Grass Valley is the fabled Empire Mine. This Rolls Royce of gold mines operated from 1850 to 1956, and during that time produced gold worth in excess of $2 billion at today's prices. The mine's tunnels eventually went as deep as 11,000 feet and extended for 367 miles. The highlights are the Willis Polk-designed mine owner's mansion — the Bourn Cottage — and the mine itself, where you can peer into the entrance and see two sets of rails leading deep into the earth.

Malakoff Diggins State Historic Park, (916) 265-2740. Roughly 20 miles north of Nevada City and off the beaten path is the starkly beautiful Malakoff Diggins. The scene of hydraulic gold mining in the 19th century, in which large water cannons called monitors washed away whole hillsides in search of gold, the area today is a sandy waste of exposed mounds banded in colors ranging from bright white to ochre to rust red.

There is a multitude of other attractions in the gold country, too numerous to mention here. Contact the various counties' chambers of commerce, listed below, for further information.

Phones: Tuolumne County Chamber of Commerce, 55 W. Stockton Rd., Sonora, (209) 532-4212; Amador County Chamber of Commerce, 2048 W. Highway 88, Jackson, (209) 223-0350; Calaveras County Chamber of Commerce, 1301 S. Main St., Angels Camp, (209) 736-2875; El Dorado County Chamber of Commerce, 542 Main St., Placerville, (916) 621-5885; Nevada County/Grass Valley Area Chamber of Commerce, 248 Mill St., Grass Valley, (916) 273-4667.
Hours: All the parks are open daily from approximately 10 a.m. to 5 p.m. from Memorial Day to Labor Day; other times of the year it's more likely to be weekends only. Phone ahead to check.
Admission: Columbia State Historic Park is free. Empire Mine charges $2.00 for adults and $1.00 for children (6–12). The other three parks charge day-use fees of $5.00 per vehicle.
Wheelchair Access: Malakoff Diggins and parts of the Empire Mine are not wheelchair accessible. The other three parks are.

Lake Tahoe

Located 195 miles northeast of San Francisco via Highways 80 or 50.

Nestled in an evergreen forest high in the Sierra Nevada, this large alpine lake is one of the most beautiful in the world. At 1,645 feet deep — the second deepest in the U.S. — it is 22 miles long and 12 miles wide. The lake straddles the California-Nevada border; two-thirds of it is in California, one-third in Nevada.

Lake Tahoe has 71 miles of shoreline, and you could easily drive around it in a few hours. Though the drive is scenic you would miss much of what the region offers if you never got out of your car.

South Lake Tahoe, at the south end of the lake, is the area's "metropolis." Starting from the intersection of Highway 89 and 50, if you head east on 50 — Lake Tahoe Boulevard — the next five miles will take you through the heart of the business district and past scores of shops, restaurants, and motels. The motels are particularly numerous just west of Stateline, the appropriately named first town on the Nevada side of the border.

Before crossing into Nevada, however, there are two worthwhile attractions, both of them scenic ways to see the lake itself. Ski Run Boulevard, four miles east of the "Y" intersection of 89 and 50, leads to both of them. Left on Ski Run toward the lake will take you to the dock where the **Tahoe Queen**, (800) 238-2463, paddlewheel boat docks. This glassbottomed boat provides daily excursions of the lake all year long (the lake never freezes over). If you turn right on Ski Run Boulevard, toward the mountains, and then follow the signs, you'll come to to **Heavenly Valley**, open year round, (702) 586-7000, the most notable ski resort in the area. An aerial tramway here takes you 2,000 feet up the mountainside to the Top of the Tram restaurant, where there is a panoramic view of the lake and the surrounding mountains.

Continuing east on Lake Tahoe Boulevard you will have no trouble discerning the state line as you drive into Nevada. **Stateline** greets you with two huge highrise hotel/casinos —

Harvey's on your left and Harrah's on your right. While not the gambling mecca that Las Vegas is, Stateline offers plenty of action in these and other hotel/casinos in the immediate vicinity.

Continue north on 50 until you reach the intersection of Highway 28. Take a left to continue your circuit of the lake. Toward the north end of the lake you will pass through **Lake Tahoe Nevada State Park.** Although the Nevada side of the lake is less scenic than the California side, the Sand Point peninsula offers nice views of the lake, along with swimming and picnic areas.

Less than a mile up the road after leaving the park you will come to the **Ponderosa Ranch,** site of the popular 1960s TV series "Bonanza." You can visit the Cartwright's ranch house and the adjacent re-created western town.

While you are in the area, several scenic detours beckon. From Incline Village on the Nevada side of the lake's north shore, Highway 431 — the Mount Rose Highway — will take you over the mountains to Highway 395.

North on 395 takes you to **Reno,** the second largest city in Nevada (and another gambling mecca); south takes you to **Virginia City,** site of the "Big Bonanza," the great silver rush of the 1860s and 1870s. Virginia City is now kept alive solely by tourism, but that is enough; the flavor of the Old West lingers strong here. Many buildings still remain from as far back as the 1870s, including Piper's Opera House and the offices of the *Territorial Enterprise,* the newspaper where Mark Twain got his start as a writer.

Back at Lake Tahoe, Highway 28 east takes you around the lake's north shore. At Crystal Bay you'll cross back into California. The small lakeside communities that you'll pass — such as Kings Beach, Agate Bay, and Lake Forest — consist mainly of seasonal vacation homes.

At the intersection of Highways 28 and 89 is the largest town on the north shore, **Tahoe City** (population 5,000). There is a nice public beach, accessible across from 510 North Lake Boulevard. Just past Highway 89 as you head south along the west shore you will cross Fanny Bridge spanning the Truckee River, the lake's only outlet.

Nine miles south of Tahoe City is one of the three major state parks on the California side, **Sugar Pine Point State Park**, (916) 525–7982; (916) 525–7232 (winter). The highlight here, just a stone's throw from the water, is the **Ehrman Mansion**, the summertime home of a wealthy San Francisco family during the 1920s. Nearby are the estate's stables, servants' quarters, boat-houses, and other buildings. The tree-shaded park has picnic areas and hiking trails.

A short distance south of Sugar Pine is **D. L. Bliss State Park**, which has a large campground, and immediately adjoining it to the south is **Emerald Bay State Park**. Just off the main parking lot is an overlook that provides a grand view of what has been called "the most beautiful inland harbor in the world." Emerald Bay gets its name from its emerald green color, which is in contrast to the deep blue of the rest of the lake.

A highlight at Emerald Bay is **Vikingsholm**, (916) 525-7277, a replica of an ancient Viking castle. Built of stone, mortar, and wood, this former mansion of a wealthy heiress is replete with Scandinavian period pieces and wood carvings. The house's interior is open for tours only from June through August.

Phones: South Lake Tahoe Chamber of Commerce, 3066 Lake Tahoe Blvd., South Lake Tahoe, (916) 541-5255; Lake Tahoe Visitors Authority (at South Lake Tahoe), (916) 544-5050; North Lake Tahoe Chamber of Commerce, 245 North Lake Blvd., Tahoe City, (916) 581-6900; Tahoe North Visitors & Convention Bureau, 950 North Lake Blvd., Tahoe City, (916) 583-3494. Ponderosa Ranch, 100 Ponderosa Ranch Road, Incline Village, NV, (702) 831-0691.
Hours: All the parks are open daily subject to weather conditions. The Ehrman mansion offers tours daily on the hour 11 a.m. to 4 p.m., July - September only. Vikingsholm offers tours daily 10 a.m. to 4 p.m., June - August only. The Ponderosa Ranch is open May through October, 9:30 a.m. to 5 p.m.
Admission: Lake Tahoe Nevada and Sugar Pine Point state parks charge $5.00 per vehicle for use of the facilities. Tahoe Queen: Adults $14.00; Children (under 12) $5.00; reservations required. Heavenly Valley: Adults $12.00; Children $6.50; under 3, Free. Vikingsholm: Adults $2.00; Children (6–17) $1.00. Ponderosa Ranch: Adults $8.50; Children (5–11) $5.50; under 5, Free.
Wheelchair Access: Call individual locations for specific information.

Mendocino

On Highway 1, 150 miles northwest of San Francisco.

Mendocino is a charming seacoast hamlet that resembles a 19th-century New England whaling village. Its ambience and its many bed-and-breakfast inns make it a favorite spot for a romantic getaway. The town also abounds with art and craft galleries.

The best weather here is generally to be found in the autumn, but if you are visiting in the winter or spring a big attraction is **whale-watching**. From mid-December through April, California gray whales migrate down the coast, then up, all the while putting on a free show by shooting plumes of water in the air when they exhale, flipping their flukes before diving, or occasionally bursting from the water before crashing with a giant splash.

Since the whales stay close to shore (particularly in the spring) you can see them from the coastal bluffs. For those who want a closer look, charter boats are available.

Mendocino has a number of historic houses, several of which have been turned into museums. The **Ford House,** dating from 1854, (707) 937-5397, on the south side of Main Street, has an interpretive center that provides information on the area's natural environment. Other exhibits chart the history of Mendocino starting with the Native Americans.

Across the street and a block down is the **Kelley House Museum,** (707) 937-5791. Its display cases hold women's Victorian-era dresses and jewelry.

Fort Bragg, located 10 miles north on Highway 1, is a lumber mill town — as was Mendocino in its early days. It's a throwback to the 1950s, appearing to have changed little since then. There are plenty of motels here at both ends of town, many with reasonable rates.

A main attraction here is the **Skunk Train** (the depot is at Laurel Avenue, just west of Main Street), (707) 964-6371, whose official name is the California Western Railroad. It makes trips daily between the coast and Willits, inland on Highway 101, chugging through a redwood forest at up to 20 miles per hour. Half- and full-day trips are offered. For a more authentic train experience choose the steam engine train over the gasoline powered one if you have the opportunity.

Next to the railroad depot, the **Guest House Museum,** (707) 961-2825, tells the history of Fort Bragg's timber industry, using historic photos and artifacts.

A block away on Franklin Street, next to the city hall, is the **Fort Building,** the only structure remaining from the original 1857 army post for which the town is named. It houses a small museum with models and photos of the fort.

Plant- and nature-lovers will enjoy the **Mendocino Coast Botanical Gardens,** (707) 964-4352. Located two miles south of Fort Bragg on the ocean side of Highway 1, it offers a network of trails through rhododendrons, wildflowers, fuschias, and other flora.

Half a dozen state parks and reserves dot the coastline in the area. They offer beaches and trails and the opportunity to relax and enjoy the rugged beauty of the Mendocino coast.

Phone: Mendocino Coast Chamber of Commerce, 332 N. Main St., Ft. Bragg, (707) 961-6300.
Hours: The Skunk Train operates daily. Call for schedule and reservations. The Botanical Garden is open daily, 9 a.m. to 5 p.m. The museums mentioned above are only open certain days, with restricted hours.
Admission: The museums mentioned are either free or cost no more than $1.00. Admission to the Botanical Garden ranges from $3.00 to $5.00. Skunk Train fares for half-day and one-way trips are: Adults $21.00, Children $12.00; for full-day roundtrips it is Adults $26.00, Children $12.00. Children under 5 who sit on their parents laps ride free.
Wheelchair Access: The Skunk Train, the Botanical Garden, and all the museums except for the second floor of the Kelley House in Mendocino, and the Fort Building in Fort Bragg, are wheelchair accessible.

Monterey and Carmel

Located on the California coast, 125 miles south of San Francisco.

The Monterey peninsula has the most scenic, picturesque stretch of coastline in the state of California. Wind-sculpted cypress trees overlook rock-strewn coves and inlets that alternate with the occasional patch of South Pacific-like white sand beach. Author Robert Louis Stevenson described this area as "the greatest meeting of land and water in the world."

Monterey is not only scenic but historic as well. Still standing are more than 40 adobes and other buildings dating from 1795 to the late 1840s — a period when first Spain, then Mexico, and finally the U.S., claimed Monterey as the capital of California.

The **Path of History Walking Tour** (self-guiding or docent led) helps bring this era alive. Highlights include: the Custom House, the interior of which is stocked with goods re-creating the Mexican era of the 1830s and 40s; the Old Whaling Station, whose front sidewalk is composed of whale vertebrae; the Larkin House, the graciously-furnished home of Thomas O. Larkin, the first and only U.S. consul to Mexican California; Colton Hall, where California's constitutional convention of 1849 was held.

Many of the locations carry the tour map; you can start anywhere. But the best place to begin is in the Custom House area. Docent-led tours start at the Stanton Center, just steps from the Custom House itself.

Adjoining the Stanton Center is the new **Maritime Museum**, 5 Custom House Plaza, (408) 373-2469. This museum provides a fine introduction to Monterey and its history. Spread across two floors is a wealth of artifacts covering everything from the first Spanish landing, in 1602, through the heyday of Cannery Row.

A mile to the northwest of the historic downtown is **Cannery Row**. Immortalized by John Steinbeck in his novel of the same name, this street, in the early decades of the 20th century, was home to numerous sardine canneries. The once plentiful sardines are long gone and so are many of the buildings, but the remaining packing plants and warehouses have been converted into shops and waterfront restaurants.

At the north end of Cannery Row is a spectacular recent addition, the **Monterey Bay Aquarium**, (408) 648-4800. Monterey's most popular single attraction, this huge aquarium draws nearly two million visitors a year. All of the exhibits focus on some aspect of the rich marine life of Monterey Bay.

Major permanent exhibits include the Kelp Forest, which is stocked with sardines, sharks, and other fish. At 28 feet high it is the tallest aquarium exhibit in the world. Monterey Bay Habitats, a 90-foot-long pool, re-creates four different bay environments ranging from deep reefs to the shallow wharf area. Sea otters are one of the more popular attractions; crowds gather to watch these cute creatures frolic.

Anchoring the southern end of the peninsula is the charming town of **Carmel**. Founded as an artists' colony, it is now one of the choicest communities in the state. Ocean Avenue, the main street, is lined with elegant shops. At the end of Ocean Avenue there is a beautiful white sand beach framed by Monterey Cypress trees.

A mile and a quarter south on Scenic Drive is **Tor House**, (on Ocean View Avenue near Stewart Way), (408) 624-1813, the home of California poet Robinson Jeffers. Constructed in 1919, this enchanting cottage was built of stones hauled up from the beach. The house's cozy living room with its central fireplace, low ceiling, and its sitting-level window with a view of the ocean would bring out the poet in anyone.

A few blocks inland is **Carmel Mission**, on Rio Road near Highway 1, (408) 624-3600. It was founded in 1770 by Fray Junipero Serra, father of the Franciscan missions in California. Serra is buried under the rebuilt floor of the chapel. The former padres' quarters now houses a museum packed with unique artifacts, including a number of items associated with Serra. You can also see a lance and leather shield owned by a soldier who accompanied the Portolà expedition up the California coast — the one that led to the discovery of San Francisco Bay.

Two miles south of the mission via Highway 1 is the wildly beautiful **Point Lobos State Reserve**, (408) 624-4909. This rugged peninsula, jutting unexpectedly into Carmel Bay, is chock-a-block with scenic coves — so scenic that quite a number of movies have been filmed here, including Alfred Hitchcock's *Rebecca* and the original *Treasure Island*, starring Wallace Beery and Lionel Barrymore. A museum at Whalers Cove provides a good orientation. Also note parts of a whale skeleton on the ground outside — a skull and some ribs and vertebrae.

If you'd rather see scenery from the comfort of your car, the **17-mile Drive** winding through the exclusive Pebble Beach area can't be beat. You'll pass by million-dollar homes as well as several of the finest golf courses in the country. A good portion of the drive hugs the picturesque coastline. The famous "Lone Cypress," a single tree hugging a rocky promontory, can be found near the southern end of the drive.

Phones: Monterey State Historic Park office, 20 Custom House Plaza, Monterey, (408) 649-7118; Monterey Peninsula Chamber of Commerce and Visitor and Convention Bureau, 350 Alvardo Street, Monterey, (408) 649-1770; Carmel Business Association, corner San Carlos Street and 7th Avenue, Carmel, (408) 624-2522.

Hours: The buildings on the Path of History Walking Tour have widely varying hours. The Custom House and Maritime Museum are open daily, 10 a.m. to 4 p.m. and 5 p.m. respectively; almost all the others are open only certain days. Monterey Bay Aquarium is open daily, 10 a.m. to 6 p.m. Tor House is open Friday and Saturday, 10 a.m. to 4 p.m.; reservations are advised. Carmel Mission is open daily, 9:30 a.m. to 4:30 p.m.; Sundays from 10:30 a.m. Point Lobos State Reserve is open daily, 9 a.m. to 5 p.m.; to 7 p.m. in the summer.

Admission: On the self-guided Monterey Path of History most of the buildings offer free admission; a few charge $2.00 per person. Docent-led tours cost $2.00 plus $2.00 additional for entrance to certain buildings, or $5.00 will buy you a two-day pass good for admission to all buildings. The Maritime Museum charges from $5.00 for adults to $2.00 for children. Monterey Bay Aquarium fees range from $10.50 for adults to $4.75 for children. Tor House costs $5.00 per person. Carmel Mission fee is $1.00 per person. Point Lobos State Reserve and the 17-mile Drive both cost $6.00 per vehicle.

Wheelchair Access: Accessibility of the buildings on the Monterey Path of History is usually confined to the first floor. The Maritime Museum is fully accessible as is the Monterey Bay Aquarium. Tor House is not accessible. The Carmel Mission is accessible except for one or two rooms. Point Lobos State Reserve offers only limited access on its dirt trails.

Russian River Resort Area

Located 75 miles northwest of San Francisco.

The Russian River region, with its quaint homes and cabins nestled among the redwoods, has served as a resort area and weekend getaway spot for San Franciscans since the 1940s. Several waves of "settlers" have come and gone since then. In the 1960s and 1970s it was first bikers, then hippies; gays established a presence in the 1980s.

Today there is a varied population, and the region offers a little something for everyone — hiking, bicycling, wine tasting, canoeing down the river, or just plain relaxing. River Road, from just north of Forestville, follows the river west to the sea. It's a pretty drive through the redwoods: in some places you will see vineyards planted practically to the river's edge.

The major town along the route is **Guerneville**. This is the best place to have lunch or pick up picnic supplies. Stop at the visitor center, 4034 Armstrong Woods Road, (707) 253-8800, for brochures and maps.

Just a little over two miles farther north on Armstrong Woods Road is the **Armstrong Redwoods State Reserve**, (707) 869-2015 or (707) 865-2391, a primeval forest and the home of the last stand of old-growth redwoods in Sonoma County. Soaring high above the streamside forest floor of ferns and clover are some towering specimens. A few are over 300 feet high and over 1,300 years old.

If you return to Guerneville and head west on Highway 116 for eight miles you will come to the town of **Duncans Mills**. Once the site of a redwood lumber mill, the town now caters to the tourist trade; it's chock-a-block with art galleries and gift shops. The restored railroad depot is open Saturdays at 10 a.m. for tours.

Four miles west of Duncans Mills you will reach the coast and the town of **Jenner,** situated on a bluff overlooking the mouth of the placid Russian River. During the summer you may see seal pups cavorting in the river.

The broad sand beach that stretches south from the river's mouth along the coast is part of **Goat Rock State Beach**, one of the more accessible beaches along this part of the coast. The entrance is less than a mile south of Jenner on Highway 1.

A worthwhile side trip is a visit to **Fort Ross**, (707) 847-3286, 11 miles north of Jenner on Highway 1. This restored and reconstructed wooden fort, surrounded by a stockade, was originally built by Russian settlers in 1812. The Russians had come this far south to hunt sea otters and to grow wheat and other crops to help support their colonies in Alaska. You are free to explore the commandant's house, the barracks, the chapel, and other structures to learn more about this little-known aspect of California history.

If you return to Jenner and continue south on Highway 1 for another 11 miles you will come to the town of **Bodega Bay**. The drive before you get there is a beautiful one; the road winds along above high cliffs that drop off sharply to the ocean below. There are many state beaches along the route, and in a few places houses dramatically hug the cliffs just above the beach.

Bodega Bay is an attractive town with a protected harbor. It offers sport fishing, horseback riding, and golf, to go along with beautiful views of the bay and the ocean. The visitor center, 850 Coast Highway 1 (just south of the Unocal gas station), (707) 875-3422, can provide further information.

A few miles farther south on Highway 1 will bring you to the small town of **Bodega** — turn left on Bodega Highway. With its Victorian Gothic schoolhouse and church Bodega looks as if time stopped here over a century ago.

Directions: From Highway 101, take the River Road exit; farther south from 101, Highway 12 to Sebastopol and then Highway 116 north to Forestville is an alternate route.
Hours: Armstrong Redwoods State Reserve is open 8 a.m. to one hour after sunset. Fort Ross is open 10 a.m. to 4:30 p.m.
Admission: Armstrong Redwoods is free if you walk in; $5.00 per vehicle if you drive in. Fort Ross costs $5.00 per vehicle.
Wheelchair Access: Armstrong Redwoods: some trails are paved and accessible; Fort Ross: the ground in the fort is uneven and bumpy but the visitor center is fully accessible.

Sacramento

Sacramento is 85 miles northeast of San Francisco via Highway 80.

Although not on a par with Yosemite and the Monterey Bay area as tourist and weekend-getaway locations, Sacramento does have a number of attractions that make it worth a visit.

The place to start is **Old Sacramento**, on the east bank of the Sacramento River between I Street and Capitol Mall, (916) 264-7777 or 442-7644. Considered to have the finest collection in the country of historic buildings in such a concentrated area, Old Sacramento today has been restored to its late 19th-century appearance. A magnet for tourists, its storefronts now house numerous ice cream parlors, gift shops, and restaurants instead of hardware stores and wholesale grocers.

Old Sacramento is also home to several museums. A must see is the **California State Railroad Museum**, 111 I Street, (916) 448-4466. The largest railroad museum in the United States, it houses 21 beautifully-restored locomotives and cars dating from the 1860s to the 1960s. Highlights include the gleaming Governor Stanford engine from the Central Pacific Railroad and a Pullman sleeping car that vividly re-creates overnight train travel.

A few doors down is the **Sacramento History Museum**, 101 I Street, (916) 264-7057. Located in a reconstruction of the 1854 City Hall, its wealth of artifacts charts the history of Sacramento from the time of the Native Americans up to the present.

A few blocks to the east is the **State Capitol**, 10th Street between L and N streets, (916) 324-0333. Constructed in the 1860s and 1870s, it was earthquake proofed and had its interior restored to its turn-of-the-century appearance in 1982. The former ground floor offices have been re-created as period rooms — such as the 1906 governor's office, complete with spittoon on the floor.

Sutter's Fort State Historic Park, 2701 L Street, (916) 445-4422, is a reconstruction of the fort built by pioneer John Sutter in the 1840s. Sutter, a Swiss emigré, was the first European to settle in the Sacramento valley. His fort was the destination for the ill-fated

Donner party, and was also where John Marshall brought the first gold nuggets that he discovered at Coloma in 1848.

Located on the same block as Sutter's Fort is the **California State Indian Museum**, 2816 K Street, (916) 324-0971. On display are numerous photographs and artifacts documenting the culture and lives of California Indians. A particular strength is the large collection of Indian baskets.

Any art lover will want to visit the **Crocker Art Museum**, 216 O Street, (916) 264-5423. This oldest public art museum in the West houses more than 700 European and American paintings. Of particular interest are some fine 19th-century California landscapes by Thomas Hill and William Keith. The beautiful Victorian interior of this mansion serves as the perfect backdrop for these and other works. The museum also has a growing collection of post-1945 paintings and sculpture by northern California artists.

The **Governor's Mansion**, 16th and H streets, (916) 445-1209, built in 1877, was the home of 13 California governors, starting in 1903. Ronald Reagan was the last to inhabit it; the house today looks much as it did when he and his family moved to a new governor's mansion in 1967.

The **Leland Stanford Mansion State Historic Park**, 8th and N streets, (916) 324-0575, offers visitors a rare chance to see a historic house in the process of restoration. Leland Stanford was one of the Big Four, the quartet of entrepreneurs who built the western half of the first transcontinental railroad. Docent-led tours provide a look at the progress being made on restoring this mansion to its 1860s appearance. Call first; tours are given irregularly.

Hours: All are open daily at least 10 a.m. to 5 p.m. except the Sacramento History Museum and the Crocker Art Museum, which are closed Mondays and Tuesdays. The Stanford Mansion is open on an irregular basis. Call for the schedule.
Admission: The State Capitol and the Stanford Mansion are free. The California State Railroad Museum charges $5.00 for adults and lesser amounts for seniors and children. The other attractions cost $3.00 or less.
Wheelchair Access: With the exception of the upper floors of the Governor's Mansion, all are wheelchair accessible.

Santa Cruz

Located on the California coast, 70 miles south of San Francisco.

Santa Cruz, at the north end of Monterey Bay, is home to the finest beaches in northern California. Its coastline is quite scenic, although it lacks the rugged beauty of the Monterey peninsula.

Santa Cruz's central attraction is its historic **Boardwalk**, 400 Beach Street, (408) 426-7433. The only remaining major amusement park along the California coast, it is home to 27 rides, including the classic Big Dipper roller coaster, which dates from 1924. Concrete has replaced the original *board* walk, but the park still exudes summertime fun — roller coasters, merry-go-rounds, games of skill, cotton candy, ice cream cones. In front of the Boardwalk is a beautiful expanse of white sand beach.

The coastal waters off Santa Cruz have been a surfing mecca since the 1930s. The **Santa Cruz Surfing Museum**, Lighthouse Point, off West Cliff Drive, (408) 429-3429, housed in a former lighthouse hugging the coast, charts this sport's history (which dates back to 15th-century Hawaii). Among the artifacts on display are lots of old photographs, and surfboards from antique to modern, including a recent one bearing tooth marks of a Great White shark.

Farther north along the coast is the **Long Marine Lab**, end of Delaware Avenue, (408) 459-2883, a U.C. Santa Cruz facility that conducts research on the local marine life. A small visitor center/aquarium at the entrance has tanks brimming with fish and shellfish native to the area. In the courtyard just behind the aquarium is a complete skeleton of the largest creature on earth — a blue whale. On occasion you may be able to watch local scientists work with seals or sea lions in holding tanks on the grounds.

Also along the coast, but south of the Boardwalk, is the **Santa Cruz Museum of Natural History**, 1305 East Cliff Drive (at Pilkington), (408) 429-3773. A sure attention getter here is a mastodon skull that was found in a nearby creek in 1980. Also of interest is a fine display of artifacts from the local Ohlone Indians, including a quite rare Ohlone basket (only about a dozen are known to exist).

In the heart of downtown you will find one of the city's newest cultural attractions, the **Art Museum of Santa Cruz County**, 705 Front Street, (408) 454-0697. This very attractive museum features changing exhibitions of art and photography. A separate history gallery has appealing exhibits on the history of Santa Cruz, including a fine rendering of its development as a beach resort in the early 1900s.

If you are a history buff you'll want to see the only remaining building from the early **Mission Santa Cruz**, end of School Street (off Emmet), (408) 425-5849, an eight-room adobe dating from 1824. This small state historic park does a better job than any other comparable one of conveying how the people of the time lived. The artifacts and informative panels in each room chart how first the Native Americans and later the Hispanic and Irish residents moved into these rooms and changed them to fit their lifestyles. One room is re-created as an archeological dig-in-progress. It gives one the sensation of having made a wonderful discovery to see such things as the finger marks left by a Native American.

Just a few miles south of Santa Cruz is the seaside town of **Capitola**. Of most interest is the picturesque beach area. A pedestrian esplanade winds past colorful, stuccoed cottages and alongside popular waterfront bars and restaurants. The commercial district nearby is noted for its fine arts and crafts shops.

Up in the hills east of Highway 1 is a most unusual attraction — the **Mystery Spot**, 1953 Branciforte Drive, Santa Cruz, (408) 423-8897. Here, in a 150-foot circle in the forest, some strange gravitational pull causes people to feel dizzy and to tilt at odd angles. Compasses go haywire, birds avoid the area, and balls roll uphill! Although your guide will offer some theories as to what causes all this, it still remains an unexplained phenomenon.

Eight miles inland amidst a redwood forest is an attraction that children, especially, will enjoy — **Roaring Camp & Big Trees Narrow-Gauge Railroad**, (408) 335-4484. A remnant of an earlier time, a steam-driven locomotive pulling open-air passenger cars takes visitors through a redwood forest, all the while spewing plumes of steam into the tree branches above. The station area, which has plenty of picnic tables, looks like a Hollywood movie set with its re-created 1880s-era general store and other buildings.

Next to Roaring Camp is **Henry Cowell Redwoods State Park**, (408) 335-4598. Several trails loop through the park and take you past some awesome redwoods, a few of which are over 1,000 years old.

Phone: Santa Cruz County Conference and Visitors Council, 701 Front Street, Santa Cruz, (408) 425-1234.
Hours: The Boardwalk is open daily; call for current hours. Santa Cruz Surfing Museum is open Thursday - Monday, Noon to 4 p.m. Long Marine Lab is open Tuesday - Sunday, 1 to 4 p.m. The Museum of Natural History's hours are Tuesday - Friday, 10 a.m. to 5 p.m.; weekends 1 to 5 p.m. The Art Museum is open Tuesday - Sunday, 11 a.m. to 4 p.m. The Mission Santa Cruz adobe is open Thursday - Sunday, 10 a.m. to 4 p.m. The Mystery Spot is open daily, 9:30 a.m. to 5 p.m. Roaring Camp Railroad is open daily during the summer; call for the train schedules and off-season days and hours. Henry Cowell State Park is open daily from dawn to dusk.
Admission: The Boardwalk itself is free of charge; rides cost anywhere from $0.50, to $16.95 for an all-day pass. Roaring Camp Railroad costs $11.50 for adults and $8.50 for children (3–15). Henry Cowell State Park charges $5.00 per vehicle. Long Marine Lab is free; all the other attractions charge $3.00 or less for adults, and lesser amounts for seniors and children.
Wheelchair Access: All are accessible except for the Mystery Spot. The Surfing Museum has two small steps leading to it.

Wine Country – Napa Valley

The Napa Valley starts about 40 miles northeast of San Francisco.

America's most celebrated wine region, the Napa Valley is home to almost 250 wineries. Many of them welcome visitors and offer tours and tastings. Some wineries charge for tastings (up to $5.00 per person), but most don't.

Part of the vineyard experience is in visiting the grounds themselves. Winery mansions range from quaint Victorians to stone castles to modernistic architect-designed estates. Surprisingly, only a few wineries provide picnic areas.

You don't have to love wine to enjoy visiting this scenic valley. There are other attractions that make it worth a visit.

The place to start is the town of **Napa** itself, on Highway 29. Stop at the visitor center downtown — take the First Street exit and follow the signs to 1310 Napa Town Center, (707) 226-7459. Here you can pick up winery touring maps as well as brochures on other attractions.

Within walking distance of the visitor center is the **Napa County Historical Society Museum**, 1219 First Street, (707) 224-1739. It's mainly a research library, but on display are artifacts related to the Napa Valley's history — Indian baskets, period clothing, old pistols, etc.

Heading north from Napa up Highway 29 or the Silverado Trail (the latter drive is especially scenic) will take you past a host of wineries to the charming town of St. Helena, 18 miles distant. At the south end of town on the west side of Highway 29 is the **Napa Valley Museum**, 473 First Street, (707) 963–7411. Housed in the former high school, this attractive museum has exhibits and artifacts on the local Indians, early settlers, mining resorts, and, of course, viticulture.

Also in St. Helena, two blocks east of the main street, is the **Silverado Museum**, 1490 Library Lane, (707) 963-3757. This museum is dedicated solely to author Robert Louis Stevenson, who spent his honeymoon in the Napa Valley in 1880. Glass cases contain such things as Stevenson's wedding ring, toy soldiers he played with as a boy, and first editions of his books.

Just three and four miles respectively farther north on the west side of Highway 29 are two state parks — the **Bale Grist Mill**, (707) 963-2236, and the **Bothe-Napa Valley**, (707) 942-4575. Bale Grist Mill is an 1846 water-powered mill that was used for grinding corn, wheat, and other grains. Completely restored, the water wheel turns everyday; demonstrations of actually grinding various grains are held less frequently. Bothe-Napa Valley State Park offers hiking, picnicking, and camping. It is one of the few state parks that has a swimming pool (open summers only).

Calistoga, the last major town at the north end of the Napa Valley, is a resort area noted for the local hot springs. Spas and motels on Lincoln Avenue and several side streets offer various mud baths, mineral baths, and massages.

Also of interest in Calistoga is the **Sharpsteen Museum**, 1311 Washington Street, (707) 942-5911. It covers the history of Calistoga. A highlight is a diorama of the initial elaborate resort built by town founder Sam Brannan. One of the original cottages from that 1860s resort constitutes the east end of the museum.

For more information on things to do in the Calistoga area stop by the visitor center located at the historic railroad station, 1458 Lincoln Avenue, (707) 942-6333. They have many brochures on accommodations, spas, wineries, and other attractions.

Less than a mile north of Calistoga, on the left side of the highway, is the Petrified Forest Road which, as the name implies, leads to **The Petrified Forest**, (about five miles from Calistoga), (707) 942-6667. This privately-owned attraction is home to the largest petrified trees in the world. Here you will see some giant redwoods lying flat after having been felled by a volcanic eruption nearly three million years ago. They are remarkably life-like except for the fact that they have turned to stone.

Return to Highway 29, continue farther north a short distance, take a right on Tubbs Lane, and you will come to **Old Faithful Geyser**, 1299 Tubbs Lane, (707) 942-6463. Geothermal activity is what accounts for all of the area's hot springs; here you can see an example in action. It is one of the few geysers in the world that erupts on such a regular schedule — about every 40 minutes, although that can lengthen to as much as an hour and a quarter.

If you enjoy hiking, a final nearby attraction (continue north five miles on Highway 29) is **Robert Louis Stevenson Memorial State Park**, (707) 942-4575. A trail leading from the highway will take you to the site of the cabin where Stevenson and his bride spent their honeymoon. Continue farther on the trail and you will reach the summit of Mount St. Helena, from which on clear days there are spectacular views.

Hours: You can generally count on all the attractions mentioned above as being open at least from 10 a.m. to 4 p.m. daily during the summer. Call first.
Admission: The Silverado and Sharpsteen museums and Robert Louis Stevenson State Park are free.
Bothe-Napa Valley State Park has a day use fee of $5.00; adult admissions for the others range between $2.00 and $4.50.
Wheelchair Access: All the above are wheelchair accessible except for the Napa Valley Museum and Robert Louis Stevenson State Park. The Petrified Forest has partial access.

Wine Country – Sonoma

The town of Sonoma is 35 miles north of San Francisco.

Sonoma County lies just west of the Napa Valley. It is also home to hundreds of wineries. Sonoma, in fact, claims to be the birthplace of the California wine industry, since it was Franciscan priests who, in the 1820s, planted the first vineyards, in order to produce sacramental wines.

The focal point of this region is the historic town of Sonoma — specifically, the Plaza and its surrounding buildings. You might start at the Sonoma Valley Visitors Bureau, (707) 996-1090, in the former Carnegie Library building at the Plaza's eastern edge. They have brochures and can answer any questions.

The **Plaza**, largest of its kind in the state, was laid out in 1835 by Mexican general and land baron Mariano Vallejo. Originally used as a drill field by Mexican cavalrymen, in 1846 the Plaza was the site of the Bear Flag Revolt, in which a troop of Americans descended on Sonoma, took Vallejo prisoner, and proclaimed a short-lived independent republic. A large rock in the Plaza's northeast corner marks the spot where the "Bear Flaggers" raised their crude banner. The Plaza today is a tree-studded greensward, and a lovely spot for a picnic.

Across Spain Street on the northwest corner of Spain and 1st Street East is the **Sonoma Barracks**, (707) 938-1519. This two-story adobe building was constructed between 1836 and 1841. It originally housed Mexican troops. The first room to your right, as you enter, has been re-created as a Mexican barracks complete with replica thong-laced beds, and hats, uniforms, and canteens hanging from pegs on the wall.

Next door, and worth a brief look, is the **Toscano Hotel**. Erected in 1852, the building has been restored to its turn-of-the-century appearance. You can peek inside and see the lobby with its simple bar, and a couple of poker tables spread with playing cards and shot glasses.

On the northeast corner of Spain and 1st Street East stands

Mission San Francisco Solano, (707) 938-1519, the last and northernmost of the Franciscan missions in California. The one-story adobe wing, which was built in 1825 and once housed the mission's padres, is now a museum. It has various artifacts, the most unusual of which is an old adobe brick with a cougar paw print embedded in it. The simple restored chapel, which is connected to the museum, harkens back to a time when life was less hurried.

Two blocks north of the Plaza, at 270 1st Street West, is the **Depot Park Museum**, (707) 938-1762. Its centerpiece display is a re-creation, using authentically dressed mannequins, of the raising of the Bear Flag. Also on view here are a couple of unique and arresting objects: an Indian arrowhead embedded in a human vertebra; and the feet of a grizzly bear made into a pair of boots that were worn by Ulysses S. Grant to a masked ball at the Palace Hotel in San Francisco!

Half a mile northwest of the Plaza is the **Mariano Vallejo Home**, (707) 938-1519. It is located at the end of 3rd Street; the driveway is framed by a row of mature cottonwood trees. This "Carpenter Gothic"-style house was built in 1851–52 and is set amidst lovely grounds, which include a courtyard fountain, a small vineyard, and a pond/reservoir up the hill. The house's interior is loaded with Victorian furnishings, most of them original to the house and all of them perfectly preserved.

If you have children with you you can give them a break by taking them to **Train Town**, (707) 938-3912. Located on Broadway, one mile south of the Plaza, Train Town offers rides on small-scale steam- and diesel-powered trains through a 10-acre landscaped park.

A final 'don't miss' attraction in the area is **Jack London State Historic Park**, (707) 938-5216. Located nine miles north of Sonoma, this 800-acre estate was home to author Jack London. Today, the "House of Happy Walls," a stone house built by London's widow, Charmian, is a museum. Found here is a re-creation of London's study with his desk, chair, and other furnishings, and artifacts he collected on his travels all over the world. Also of interest is a short home movie of London taken in 1916 just six days before his death.

A pleasant half-mile walk through the woods takes you to London's grave site and the ruins of "Wolf House," a grand 26-room stone and redwood mansion that mysteriously burned just before the Londons were to move into it in 1913. On another part of the property, and currently being restored, is the "Beauty Ranch Cottage," the modest house where London did his writing in later years, and where he died.

Jack London State Historic Park also has picnic tables, a network of trails, and many scenic vistas.

Directions: To reach Jack London State Historic Park from the town of Sonoma, take Highway 12 north out of town and turn left on either Agua Caliente or Madrone roads to Arnold Drive. Follow Arnold north to Glen Ellen and look for the brown and white sign on the left pointing the way to the park.
Hours: All the attractions listed above are open 10 a.m. to 5 p.m. daily, except for the Depot Park Museum, open Wednesday - Sunday, 1:30 p.m. to 4:30 p.m.
Train Town is open weekends only during the winter and spring.
Admission: The Sonoma Barracks and the Mission: Adults $2.00; Children $1.00; Under 6, Free. One admission fee is good for both attractions the same day.
Depot Park Museum: Adults $0.50; Children $0.25.
Train Town: Adults $3.50; Children $2.50.
Jack London State Historic Park: $5.00 per vehicle.
Wheelchair Access: Yes, except for the Vallejo Home.
Jack London Park is not except for the first floor of the museum.

Yosemite National Park

Located 185 miles due east of San Francisco in the Sierra Nevada.

"The only spot I have ever found that came up to the brag." So said Ralph Waldo Emerson, the 19th-century philosopher and poet, about Yosemite. From the backcountry meadows and mountains to the main valley with its dramatic rock faces and waterfalls, Yosemite is unsurpassed for spectacular scenery. A national park since 1890, it draws more than 3.5 million visitors a year.

Most visitors start by driving into Yosemite Valley, where one is greeted by views of El Capitan and Half Dome. The **Valley Visitor Center** — the closest parking lot is at Yosemite Village — has information about sights and attractions. The bookstore has a complete selection of books and maps for those who want to explore other aspects of Yosemite in depth.

Clustered near the visitor center are the park headquarters, the **Yosemite Museum**, the **Indian Cultural Exhibit**, the **Indian Village**, and the **Ansel Adams Gallery**. The latter features the photos of Ansel Adams, including his legendary pictures of Yosemite.

To really see Yosemite you have to get out of your car. Leave it at one of the parking lots (or at the hotel or campground if you are staying in the park) and take the local transportation. If you are a first-time visitor, a good orientation is to take the open-air tram, which gives a two-hour tour of the valley floor. A free and frequent shuttle bus also tours the valley, stopping at all the major sights and trailheads.

There are three relatively easy hikes from the valley floor, two of them leading to waterfalls. The closest to the visitor center is the one to **Lower Yosemite Fall**. From the Yosemite Lodge parking lot (bus stop #7) it's only a quarter of mile to the fall.

At the eastern end of the valley the most popular trail in the park is the Mist Trail, which leads to **Vernal Fall** (bus stop #16). From the trailhead it's 0.7 mile to the Vernal Fall Bridge, from where there is a stellar view of the fall. If you continue on another half mile you'll come to the top of the fall (and become wet in the process — it's not called the Mist Trail for nothing). The initial part of the trail leading to the bridge is a moderate grade; beyond that it's fairly steep.

The third hike, at the northeast end of the valley, is the one to **Mirror Lake** (bus stop #17). This is an easy half-mile trek. From the lake you'll have a good closeup view of Half Dome.

There are two main hotels in Yosemite Valley — the Ahwanhee and the Yosemite Lodge. If you're planning to stay in either of these during the summer or any weekend you will need to make reservations exactly one year in advance. The **Ahwanhee** is deluxe. Built in 1926 of large blocks of stone, it is a hotel in the grand tradition. Pay a visit even if you don't stay there. Other accomodations include Curry Village, which has hotel rooms, cabins, and tent cabins. There are several campgrounds on the valley floor and others along the Tioga Road.

If you visit during the summer be sure to drive up to **Glacier Point** (the road is closed in winter). The word "breathtaking" has become a cliche, but in this case it fits; you are perched 3,200 feet above the valley floor with a birds-eye view of the whole park. Information boards point out all the park's major landmarks and describe how glaciers created this dramatic landscape.

The other main area of the park accessible by car is Highway 120, the **Tioga Road**. The paved, two-lane road takes you through the scenic backcountry past **Tenaya Lake**, one of the largest in the park, and beautiful **Tuolumne Meadows**, where there is a visitor center. Tioga Road is open only during the summer, or from about Memorial Day to October.

Phones: Yosemite Valley Visitor Center (209) 372-0299;
Yosemite Room Reservations (209) 252-4848; Campground
Information (209) 372-0302; General Park Information
(209) 372-0264; Weather and Road Information (209) 372-4605.
Hours: The park is open everyday, 24 hours, weather permitting.
Admission: $5.00 per vehicle.
Parking: Free. There are four lots in the valley and one at Glacier Point.
Restrooms: Yes.
Wheelchair Access: The visitor centers and most parts of
Yosemite Valley are accessible.

County-by-County Recap

San Francisco

Museums

Ansel Adams Center

Asian Art Museum

Cable Car Barn and Museum

California Academy of Sciences

Cartoon Art Museum

Chinese Historical Society of America Museum

de Young Memorial Museum

Fort Mason Center museums

Jewish Museum San Francisco

Musée Mécanique

Museum of the City of San Francisco

Museum of Money of the American West

Museum of Russian Culture

National Maritime Museum

Pacific Heritage Museum

Palace of the Legion of Honor

Presidio Museum

Ripley's Believe It or Not! Museum

San Francisco Fire Department Museum

San Francisco Museum of Modern Art

San Francisco Performing Arts Library and Museum

Telephone Pioneer Communications Museum

Treasure Island Museum

Wells Fargo History Museum

Landmarks

Bay Bridge

Coit Tower

Columbarium

Conservatory of Flowers

Ferry Building

Fort Point

Golden Gate Bridge

Haas-Lilienthal House

Mission Dolores

Octagon House

Old St. Mary's Church

Palace of Fine Arts

Parks

Alamo Square

Alta Plaza

Buena Vista Park

Candlestick Park

Fort Mason

Golden Gate National Recreation Area

Golden Gate Park

Grand View Park

Japanese Tea Garden

Lafayette Park

Lake Merced and Fort Funston

Mt. Davidson

Portsmouth Square

The Presidio

Stern Grove

Strybing Arboretum and Botanical Garden

Sutro Heights Park

Twin Peaks

Washington Square

Family Attractions

Alcatraz

Cable Cars

Fisherman's Wharf

Ghirardelli Square

Hyde Street Pier

S.S. *Jeremiah O'Brien*

Lombard ("Crookedest Street") Street

U.S.S. *Pampanito*

PIER 39

San Francisco Zoo

Fun for Children

Children's Playground, Golden Gate Park

Discovery Room - California Academy of Sciences

The Exploratorium

The Jungle

Randall Museum

Neighborhoods

The Castro

Chinatown

Civic Center

The Embarcadero

Financial District

Haight-Ashbury

Jackson Square

Japantown

The Marina

The Mission District

Nob Hill

Noe Valley

North Beach

Pacific Heights

Russian Hill

South of Market

Telegraph Hill

Union Square

Union Street / Cow Hollow

Yerba Buena Gardens

Alameda County

Museums

Judah Magnes Museum

The Oakland Museum

Phoebe A. Hearst Museum of Anthropology

University Art Museum

Western Aerospace Museum

Landmarks

Camron-Stanford House

Dunsmuir House

Mission San Jose

Niles Railroad Depot

Paramount Theatre

Pardee Home

Patterson House and Ardenwood Historic Farm

Shinn House

Parks

Anthony Chabot Regional Park

Coyote Hills Regional Park

University of California Botanical Garden

Family Attractions

Jack London Square

Oakland Zoo

Fun for Children

Lawrence Hall of Science

Contra Costa County

Museums

Behring Auto Museum - Blackhawk

U.C. Berkeley Museum - Blackhawk

Landmarks

Alvarado Adobe

John Muir National Historic Site

Tao House - Eugene O'Neill National Historic Site

Parks

Black Diamond Mines Regional Preserve

Mt. Diablo

Sibley Volcanic Regional Preserve

Tilden Regional Park

Fun for Children

Lindsay Museum

Marin County

Museums

Marin Museum of the American Indian

San Quentin Prison Museum

Landmarks

Robert Dollar Mansion

Parks

Angel Island State Park

China Camp State Park

Mt. Tamalpais State Park

Muir Woods National Monument

Olompali State Historic Park

Point Reyes National Seashore

Family Attractions

Bay Model

Fun for Children

Bay Area Discovery Museum

San Mateo County

Museums

Coyote Point Museum

Landmarks

Filoli

Lathrop House

Ralston Hall

Woodside Store

Santa Clara County

Museums

Museum of American Heritage

Rosicrucian Museum

San Jose Historical Museum

San Jose Museum of Art

Tech Museum of Innovation

Landmarks

Los Altos History House

Mission Santa Clara

Villa Montalvo

Family Attractions

Great America

Winchester Mystery House

Fun for Children

Children's Discovery Museum

Palo Alto Junior Museum and Zoo

Solano County

Museums

Vallejo Naval & Historical Museum

Western Railway Museum

Family Attractions

Marine World Africa USA

Sonoma County

Landmarks

Luther Burbank Home and Gardens

Petaluma Adobe

Index